NAPOLEONIC LEADERSHIP

NAPOLEONIC LEADERSHIP

A Study in Power

STEPHANIE JONES AND JONATHAN GOSLING

Los Angeles | London | New Delhi
Singapore | Washington DC

Los Angeles | London | New Delhi
Singapore | Washington DC

SAGE Publications Ltd
1 Oliver's Yard
55 City Road
London EC1Y 1SP

SAGE Publications Inc.
2455 Teller Road
Thousand Oaks, California 91320

SAGE Publications India Pvt Ltd
B 1/I 1 Mohan Cooperative Industrial Area
Mathura Road
New Delhi 110 044

SAGE Publications Asia-Pacific Pte Ltd
3 Church Street
#10-04 Samsung Hub
Singapore 049483

Editor: Kirsty Smy
Assistant editor: Nina Smith
Production editor: Sarah Cooke
Copyeditor: Solveig Gardner Servian
Proofreader: Derek Markham
Indexer: Martin Hargreaves
Marketing manager: Catherine Slinn
Cover design: Francis Kenney
Typeset by: C&M Digitals (P) Ltd, Chennai, India
Printed and bound by CPI Group (UK) Ltd,
Croydon, CR0 4YY

Library of Congress Control Number: 2014945763

British Library Cataloguing in Publication data

A catalogue record for this book is available from
the British Library

ISBN 978-1-44629-442-0
ISBN 978-1-44629-443-7 (pbk)

At SAGE we take sustainability seriously. Most of our products are printed in the UK using FSC papers and
boards. When we print overseas we ensure sustainable papers are used as measured by the Egmont grading
system. We undertake an annual audit to monitor our sustainability.

CONTENTS

ABOUT THIS BOOK

Napoleon was a complex and contradictory character, a challenge for us to understand, despite hundreds of studies over the 200 years since his defeat at Waterloo. He had outstanding ability as a General; often his mere presence amongst the troops seemed to ensure victory. Yet his ultimate failure was on the battlefield, against an enemy provoked by his own belligerence. His charisma, energy and pragmatism won him many supporters in his military and political ambitions, but few stuck with him when things turned sour. His public appeal was gloriously affirmed in a series of plebiscites electing him to positions as Life Consul and then Emperor of the French; but the masses were to tire of his constant demands for sacrifice.

Napoleon established his own systems of patronage and reward, supposedly on post-revolutionary meritocratic ideals, but in the process he encouraged an attitude of entitlement and greed, rather than of loyalty. His attempts to temper this with fear of reprisals did not always work. His ability to manipulate, bargain and be conniving was actually surpassed by some of his closest intimates. He could suddenly seize power, but he could just as rapidly lose it. He was not concerned so much with his own lineage, but above all he wanted to create a legitimate dynasty in which his son could inherit. Always the parvenu, the adventurer, the usurper, the respect of and acceptance by the crowned heads of Europe eluded him.

Napoleon's approach to leadership provides colourful examples of how to gain and use power on the battlefield, in domestic politics, in the international scene – and in the workplace. He provides examples that are applicable to our own less turbulent times, because now the demands on leaders are just as complex and multifaceted. Strengths of Napoleonic leadership can include brilliance in a chosen field, charisma, fearlessness, adventurousness, confidence, energy, determination, passion, being visionary, and having excellent planning and organizing skills. But these can have a shadow side, such as his need for constant acclaim, demanding adulation, callously wasting resources, being too egotistical and narcissistic, being overly controlling and autocratic, manipulative, obsessive, naïve, demanding unconditional loyalty and support and focusing on self-preserving behaviours. But more important than these personal traits are the ideologies that he and others turned to in order to legitimize his power: patronage, meritocracy, charisma, force, manipulation, fear, populism and inheritance.

This book illuminates these ideologies and shows how they remain influential today. We suggest that Napoleon's attitude to these modes of operating at different times in his life helps define his leadership style and helps explain aspects of his success and ultimate failure – so in these chapters we have illustrated the manifestations of these power modes with eight episodes from Napoleon's career. There are implications here for our practical understanding of leadership, power, politics and conflict in our daily lives in our modern organizations.

HOW TO USE THIS BOOK

This book is written for people interested in power. Leadership is fundamentally about influence, which is an effect of power. It is fine to say this in theory – this book shows how it's done in practice, through the example of a maestro, Napoleon Bonaparte. We have first provided an overview of his life and career, and then more detailed case studies of eight episodes, each of which illustrates a specific way in which power is mobilised and directed. The case studies give enough detail to show what actually happened, and a sense of the human motives and responses involved. But our aim is to explain the modes of power, how they work, how they are derailed or diverted, and the inherent limits. The book is not just a collection of stories about Napoleon; it is a handbook for those concerned with leadership and power.

Each chapter works in the following way:

1. A collection of quotations from Napoleon, his contemporaries and historians.

2. A very brief summary of the themes of the chapter.

3. An episode from the life and career of Napoleon.

4. Reflections on leadership and power arising from this episode. If studying this in class or in a training course, these could be a good starting point for group discussions.

5. An essay on the mode of power that is illustrated by this episode, pointing out implications for modern organisational and political life.

6. Questions on leadership and power, to clarify the implications for people seeking greater influence in today's world.

At the end of the book, there is a short chapter called 'Executive Reflections on Leadership and Power', where experienced leaders from business and politics share their answers to some of the questions we pose.

ABOUT THE AUTHORS

Dr Stephanie Jones is Associate Professor of Organizational Behaviour at Maastricht School of Management, having graduated with a PhD from University College London, and a Bachelor's degree (in History) from the London School of Economics. Dr Jones has authored over 25 full-length internationally published books on business and management – three of them with Professor Jonathan Gosling. She teaches MBA students across the world, especially courses on leadership, culture and change. Her teaching locations include Kuwait, Egypt, Yemen, China, Vietnam, Peru, Surinam, Kazakhstan and several African countries. With a background managing businesses in recruitment, consulting, and training operations in China, India, the Middle East and Australia, Dr Jones gained extensive experience in the corporate sector before returning to academe a decade ago. She is still active in consulting and training. Dr Jones also supervises student theses, at Doctoral, Masters and Diploma level, assessing and evaluating theses around the world. *Napoleonic Leadership: a study in power* is her third book with Professor Gosling, the others being *Nelson's Way: leadership lessons from the great commander* (2005, published by Nicholas Brealey) and *Key Concepts in Leadership* (2012, also published by SAGE). Both authors are keen cruising and sometimes racing sailors, both in UK and across the world.

Professor Jonathan Gosling is Professor of Leadership at the Centre for Leadership Studies, University of Exeter, specializing in studying the leadership challenges of culturally diverse and boundary spanning organizations. His work is published in journals such as *Leadership, Harvard Business Review, Organization, Studies in Higher Education* and *Social Epistemology*. His most recent book is *Fictional Leaders: heroes, villains and absent friends* (2013, published by Palgrave Macmillan), which also includes a chapter by Dr Jones. Professor Gosling, a graduate of the Universities of East Anglia and the Cass Business School, plays a significant role in the 'greening' of management education worldwide and is co-founder of the 'One Planet MBA' at Exeter. He worked for many years as a community mediator and on other interventions inspired by psychodynamic perspectives on power and organizing. He is currently researching the leadership of malaria elimination programmes, of sustainable supply chains in China, and of professional organizations (universities, healthcare, accountancy and consultancy firms, etc.). He served as Distinguished Visiting Professor at INSEAD, France and similar roles in Canada, New Zealand and Sweden; is currently a Visiting Professor at Copenhagen Business School, a Fellow of the International Management Academy, the Windsor Leadership Trust and of the Singapore Civil Service College. He is co-founder of Coachingourselves. com and is a sailor, spouse and parent.

Visit the authors' website at: **www.napoleonic-leadership.com** for a Diagnostic Exercise, Power Questions and Chronology of Leadership.

ACKNOWLEDGEMENTS

We would like to thank our long-suffering other-halves for their patience and support and we hope they are enjoying this current hiatus of us being between books. As with all authors, we thank our publishers – a group of enthusiastic and upbeat ladies who were thrilled that we finished on time. We would also like to thank our employers – the Maastricht School of Management and University of Exeter, and latterly the Copenhagen Business School, scene of our final authors' collaborative meeting, supported by the Otto Mønsted Foundation. We are grateful to the Napoleon experts we consulted, both in print and face-to-face, especially Luca Lacitignola, an avid reader of sources in French as well as his native Italian. Getting to know Napoleon for two Brits has been a process of unlearning as well as learning, but we feel he has made a unique contribution to the study of leadership down the centuries, although that obviously was not his first intention ...

SJ, The Happy Return

JG, Exeter, Devon

July 2014

SOURCES OF QUOTATIONS FROM NAPOLEON AND HIS CONTEMPORARIES

Quotations from Napoleon and other commentators from his era appear in very many biographies and histories. We took our Napoleonic quotations (except for those cited as coming from another source) from:

Cronin, 1971, pages 88, 92, 143, 144, 264, 300

Gallo, 1997a, frontispiece and pages 1, 6, 45, 84, 85, 175, 219, 247, 279

Geyl, 1949, page 339

Markham, 1963, pages 26, 41, 42, 71, 75, 105, 111, 112, 113, 132, 133, 153, 154, 201, 202, 210 265

PRAISE FOR NAPOLEONIC LEADERSHIP

'The authors have fully capitalised on their opportunity to study one of the world's most complex and enduring leadership subjects. They provide a clever and compelling integration of well-chosen thematic historical material with sharp contemporary leadership analysis that business executives, public sector leaders and academics alike can derive a great deal of intellectual stimulation and sound practical advice from. I strongly commend this novel and delightful book.'

Brad Jackson, Head of School of Government at the Victoria University of Wellington

'A great man once said that "class is ageless". Thanks to Jones and Gosling, the leadership study that is Napoleon is ageless. Any student of leadership will come to understand the role of power, of politics, of personal charisma and of the needs of the people. Whether you are studying leadership, or doing leadership, this is a rollicking good read, and a fabulously rich text book.'

Ken Parry, Professor of Leadership Studies and co-Director of the Deakin Leadership Centre, Australia

INTRODUCTION

My mistress is power. I have given too much to its conquest to let it be taken from me, or even suffer anyone to covet it.

> To Roederer, an influential journalist, 4 November 1804

God has given me the will and the force to overcome obstacles.

> Napoleon, 1808, proclamation to the people of Madrid

The Emperor is mad and will destroy us all.

> Decres, Minister of Marine, 1806

There are many ways to power; amongst them inheritance, merit, reward or patronage, charisma, connivance, putsch, terror and election. Napoleon was master of all. His experience and the context in which he gained and kept power have much to teach us. Anyone considering how to gain a position of influence and outright power will do well to study how he did it – both the political machinations and his personal self-mastery.

His motives were complex – a mixture of personal, political and idealistic – and intertwined with his methods for holding onto power. Like any modern corporate leader, he sought to satisfy his changing needs and desires through the opportunities he discovered and created around him. Like the mining, transport and manufacturing entrepreneurs of the nineteenth and twentieth centuries, and the Internet entrepreneurs of the twenty-first century, Napoleon grabbed the instruments of power that were relevant at the time: organizations, technology and manpower.

The times were unusual. The French Revolution had swept away the monarchy, the aristocracy, the feudal system and the Church, and declared 'the rights of man', a doctrine of equality that challenged hereditary rights and championed meritocracy, but brought with it ubiquitous uncertainty about who owned property, which laws to enforce and who would do so. France was close to a general breakdown in social order. As A. J. P. Taylor said of the Russian Revolution, 'power was lying in the gutter', and in a series of moves that were bold, risky and lucky, Napoleon was one of several who simply picked it up for themselves.

Wherever he asserted his leadership, people followed him, though admittedly often because their options were limited. His charisma drew much from his strength and force of character, and much also from the desire of desperate people for a solution to the uncertainty and chaos around them.

Napoleon's grandiose vision of Europe united, of a rational, post-revolutionary world, has held sway for 200 years – and many of his dreams have been realized. A united Europe, constitutional monarchies and democratic republics are now the norm; and human rights are a basic assumption of domestic and international law.

He seized power after the destruction of the *ancien régime* and its established structures of aristocratic authority. On an unprecedented wave of optimism, many hoped that no one need any longer be locked into a fixed social position; through hard work, merit, expertise and talent, anyone could improve their standing in the new France.

Napoleon may be seen as the ideological icon of what later became the American Dream: that individual greatness might flower in the revolutionary conditions of *'liberté, egalité, fraternité'*.

Napoleon was a brilliantly successful soldier, almost undefeatable on the battlefield – and he was so much more. He oversaw the creation of a secular code of law, and the greatest modern vision of urban planning since the Romans. The impact of his early republicanism and later imperial vision was felt in the formation of the German and Italian states, in the collapse of the Ottoman and Austro-Hungarian empires, in the national assertiveness of countries in South America and arguably in radical artistic, post-classical art movements such as Romanticism and Impressionism. But he was also a despotic tyrant in the mode of Stalin, Hitler, Pinochet and Hussein; a jealous and violent misogynist, a mass-murderer and an agent of economic disaster.

Although Napoleon's approach to leadership and power was fraught with contradictions, even in decline he could raise an army for another adventure. His name is synonymous with greatness and glory – and especially the uniquely French concept of *'la Gloire'*. His reputation has survived despite his personal aggrandisement, impatience, and the blatant theft and pillage that funded his growing legions and the expansion of his empire.

Napoleon was borne on a revolutionary wave of modernism which he both exemplified and corrupted.

Napoleonic leadership was fundamentally an exercise in power. What do we mean by power, and how do we define a powerful leader? When we pick up almost any business magazine we are likely to see a survey of leaders, their power represented by symbols and metrics. We are impressed by high-profile operating and financial roles, the size and importance of the business, its health and direction, the trajectory of the leader's career and standing in the worldwide business community. Rankings refer to their thousands of employees; the billions (or trillions) of market capitalization and assets under their control; the hundreds of facilities, dozens of countries in which their businesses operate. Did the leader take the company global? Turn it around when loss-making? Beat off competitors? Create new products and services? Change its direction? Split it up and reorganize it? Make big acquisitions? Develop strategic alliances? Change the way people think? Get noticed by everyone in the world? Of course, it would be ridiculous to imagine that the leaders did all of this by themselves; but they have played a part in responding to opportunities, directing attention and energy, in harnessing the power to turn events to their will, and to determine how the story is told.

To Napoleon, power was everything, and he defined it in similar ways: the number of citizens and soldiers obeying him, the number of guns and the military hardware at his disposal, the extent of his conquered territories, the battles he won, and the changes he made in society, education, the Church, the law. He took France from post-revolutionary chaos to law, order and greatness – 'la Gloire'. He raised armies of hundreds of thousands. He alternately filled and emptied the national treasury of one of the largest countries in the Western world. His career trajectory was dramatic, from trainee gunner to emperor in two decades. He was loved or hated by millions – and even now his iconic bicorn hat is immediately recognizable, 200 years later.

We seek to explain his story by considering eight modes of power. Napoleon's career has a lot to teach us about:

- the importance of patronage to create a network of dependency and how it should be dispensed;
- the ideology of meritocracy, and the challenge of sustaining it;

- the appeal and dangers of charismatic leadership;
- the decisiveness and opportunism of seizing power in a coup d'état;
- the manipulative playing-off of enemies and allies in a form of divide and rule;
- the use and abuse of fear as a way of dominating decision making;
- the mechanisms of populism and appeals to the masses that bypass elites;
- the hopes that a leader might influence the next generation by inherited succession, the creation of a dynasty.

We will take Napoleon's career as an example of the way leaders use power to succeed in organizations and governments. The more he tasted power, the more he wanted, and became determined to possess it, for the visceral satisfaction, to make a difference to his adopted country, and to carve a niche for himself in history.

How did Napoleon get onto his meteoric trajectory, from unlikely beginnings on the island nation of Corsica, recently 'liberated' by France from Genoese occupation? Napoleon's origins were modest, he was always seen as a foreigner, and he had to use every friend he had to get a start in life. Then he had to reward them in return, as well as to constantly acknowledge family obligations. How did he develop expertise and ability, and show his potential for leadership? Napoleon was lucky enough to gain a sound training in an area of the military in which he came to excel. He was exceptionally bright and energetic, and the tumultuous times provided plenty of opportunities for this non-aristocratic outsider. The time of turmoil and absence of competition gave him his chance.

How did Napoleon make sure the powers-that-be noticed him and promoted him? His personal charisma, bravery in action and organizational abilities, and a few dramatic gestures on a stunning white horse, were risky but effective.

How did he seize the moment and make the transition from military officer to politician and statesman? First, he proved useful to the political elite by ruthlessly quelling a rebellion; later he staged – or stumbled into – a coup d'état: risky, uncertain and surprisingly effective.

What was Napoleon's approach to consensus-building as a leader? Like any ruler, often he played people off against each other. The crowned heads of Europe manoeuvred in constantly shifting alliances (and their ministers manoeuvred too, not always in concert with their sovereigns). Napoleon was part of this mix and manipulated in turn by them. He would rather be loved than feared, but was prepared to back up his 'offers' with force.

In domestic politics he imposed an increasingly severe totalitarianism, via secret police, press censorship and rigged courts. Many accepted this as the price to pay for stability and military victory – while they lasted.

Why was Napoleon so successful at attracting a popular following, even late in the day when he had abandoned two armies in the field and when Paris had already fallen and the monarchy was restored? He was able to recover from the dismal retreat from Moscow, leaving half a million men to die in the snow. His appeal – '*la Gloire*' – resonated in a unique way with his followers, and still resonates in modern France.

How did Napoleon finally lose his grip on power? It took several military defeats, the depletion of the cash reserves of the nation, the loss of a generation of soldiers, and an alliance of all the nations of Europe to beat him. And even then he had to be incarcerated far enough away to ensure that he could not make another come-back.

Here we define the power modes used by Napoleon and discussed in the pages that follow:

1. **Patronage** – The power to give favours to others, especially in ways that enhance their own power while remaining dependent or indebted to you, the power-giver.

Based on the concept of paternal and fatherly relational behaviour with offspring, patronage suggests paternalism and parental responsibility. However, it also indicates authority exercised in a way that limits individual responsibility, and is inherently unequal. The patriarch (the male head of a family or tribe) manages a patriarchy, in a society in which men have most of the power.

Closely related concepts include patrimony (property inherited from ancestors) which must be safeguarded and shared; to patronize (to treat in a condescending way; a patron) a person who gives support to chosen recipients; and ultimately patronage itself, defined as the support given by a patron. This support can be in terms of the giving of rewards, such as a benefit given in return for a service, and acts of loyalty. Ambitious people wisely choose who to follow on the basis of whom can be expected to give patronage; those with the power of patronage use it to build a base or pool of followers, and to create a sense of obligation amongst those who benefit from their patronage. Of course, the giving of gifts is one of the pleasures of power, and can bring personal satisfaction, providing worthwhile benefits and value to both parties.

Napoleon was a beneficiary of patronage in his early life (the French colonial Governor of Corsica made it possible for him to go to a military academy in mainland France, which became the crucial start to his cosmopolitan career) and Napoleon later repaid that debt by supporting France against a Corsican independence movement. In so doing, he turned against the cause once championed by his father – demonstrating the long-term effectiveness of 'debts of gratitude'. But when in power himself, Napoleon focused his use of patronage on his siblings, appointing them to positions of power and wealth. He gained little by doing so – they were already on his side, and in any case were ill-suited to the roles. Thus he used these most prominent opportunities for patronage to reward his family, rather than to extend the network of obligation and loyalty around him. But this is understandable: he wanted to ensure that the courtiers of his siblings would owe allegiance to him through them, and at the same time to avoid setting up potential rivals to his own position. And like any leader, as his power began to wane, he could offer less to his followers, the most powerful of whom shifted allegiance to the new regime when the time came.

Patronage is of critical importance to the influence wielded by any political or corporate leader: in a complex enterprise most of the work is done by people whom the leader can trust. Trust and loyalty are substantially underpinned by obligation and gratitude, which are bought by patronage.

2.   **Merit** – defined as excellence or worth, having admirable qualities, being meritorious and deserving praise. A meritocracy describes a situation or rule by people of superior talent or intellect. Merit is also a display of brilliance – a moment when a striking achievement becomes obvious.

Meritocracy depends on commonly agreed criteria of assessment, generally observable and measureable, so that it is possible to objectively examine the abilities and knowledge of a candidate, along with his or her achievements.

Napoleon was the beneficiary of a modern meritocracy from the moment he entered military academy. His progress was not dependent on family and connections, but on his educational achievements. Meritocracy was one of the rational ideals of revolutionary France, and Napoleon's ability in mathematics and geometry qualified him for the technically advanced field of artillery. At the 1793 Siege of Toulon he showed exceptional courage in battle and talent as a commander: he became 'one to watch'. His rapid promotion to General was due mainly to his proven merit as an inventive strategist as well as an inspiring leader on the battlefield. Soon he was able to demonstrate his ability to sustain long and complex campaigns, and to translate this reputation into the political sphere. Napoleon was seen as an outstanding soldier, and this great strength perhaps inevitably meant that he was less able to shine as a diplomat and peace-maker. Nonetheless, it was the Siege of Toulon, in December 1793, in which he had shone as a logistician and strategist as much as a courageous soldier – this was the launch-pad for his career.

As a leader himself, rebuilding the machinery of state, he appointed people he thought best qualified according to his dictum 'carriere ouverte aux talents' (a career open to talents). Later he initiated the first meritocratic honours system, the Legion d'Honneur, which would eventually admit over 30,000 members without reference to wealth or family background.

3. **Charisma** – the power to attract or influence, apparently an extraordinary gift, the charismatic person appears as if super-human and yet intensely present and connected. Charisma lends an ability to emotionally convince others, as if by your presence they are inspired to strive towards transcendent goals.

Patronage and merit alone were not enough to mark Napoleon out from a growing body of distinguished military officers defending France's frontiers through the crises of the Revolution. Heroic exploits, gorgeous uniforms, dramatic newspaper accounts: the anticipation must have been tremendous when Napoleon was expected on the scene. There were relatively few up-and-coming military leaders to outshine him; the aristocrats had been killed or exiled, and many of the new generation had been executed for simply choosing the wrong side in the highly unstable political situation in France.

The Italian campaign was a brilliant opportunity for Napoleon to demonstrate his courage and bravery in the field, his campaigning genius and his exceptional good luck. At the Battle of Lodi and on the Bridge of Arcola he seemed to be inspired and protected beyond normal mortals, and thus began the process of creating his legend. His tremendous work ethic and attention to detail meant that he was always a progenitor of events, and when everything else is in flux, a leader who takes initiative is immensely attractive.

Charisma is infectious: Napoleon's marshals, such as Kellerman, Ney, Murat and Junot, seemed to emanate something of the same aura; the power of the in-crowd. And charisma is enhanced by spectacle, and as Emperor Napoleon became a genius at symbolic ritual, at his coronation and weddings, but also at treaties and congresses. He harboured and honed his charisma with relentless care!

4. **Coup d'état and seizing power** – to take hold of something or someone forcibly or quickly; to take immediate advantage of an opportunity; as in a seizure, a sudden and frequently violent attack on authority – such as in a putsch – as in an unexpected and violent attempt to remove a government from power, replacing it with other leaders.

As a soldier and general, Napoleon had decisively seized opportunities, carrying them through to their uncertain conclusions. He did the same in politics: when the Directory (a committee of five) and other governmental bodies were paralysed by factions, and Napoleon's speech failed to galvanize the disputing deputies, he took it by force. The coup d'état of Brumaire (November, 1799) was not planned, yet was carried off with speed and determination. Having taken power, coordinated by his brother Lucien, Napoleon and his few supporters quickly consolidated their position by all means available: control of the media, the police, and the legislature. This did not come out of the blue: Napoleon had engineered a build-up of the pro-Bonaparte lobby for months, positioning himself for an entry into politics. On hearing of the chaotic incompetence of the Council, he abandoned his army in Egypt and dashed back to Paris to capitalize on (exaggerated) reports of his exotic victories, such as 'Bonaparte is advancing on India, and now on Constantinople ...'.

5. **Manipulation** – to handle skilfully, to control cleverly or deviously; also to connive and to condone wrongdoing in order to make gains for a greater cause; as a form of conspiring, to plan a crime together in secret, to act together as if by design or conspiracy; to be a conspirator, to act in a conspiratorial way; to get what one wants by playing people off against each other and exploiting their weaknesses.

The use of connivance and manipulation became a feature of Napoleon's way of operating after his appointment as a consul, and even when he was formally acknowledged as Emperor in 1804 he kept a tight hold of the press. He had one police service spying on another; he sent rivals on long and troublesome missions around the world; and cooked up evidence of a crime if it served his purposes. Behind all of this was the threat of force: he controlled the army, and there came a time when he no longer needed to go to the trouble of threatening people.

6. **Fear** – a feeling of distress or alarm caused by impending danger or pain, fear can manifest as a form of coercion. Terrorism excites fear of random, uncontrollable disaster, and often to fearful reaction towards leaders who offer security. There are both subtle and direct ways to use violence and intimidation to achieve political or military ends.

Managing tightly, controlling his power base, silencing critics – these became essential ways of operating, especially before he was crowned Emperor. Napoleon felt a need to know everything that was going on, to silence opposition, and to ensure complete loyalty: in short, to become a tyrant. Like most narcissists, he wanted to be adored, and would reward those who were loyal to him with loyalty in return. But those who were not admirers – even reasonable critics – he could never trust, and could be utterly ruthless towards them.

The use of fear and terror to gain and keep power became more important as he faced real and imagined threats to his dominance. Napoleon, when First Consul, had to deal with 'pretenders to the throne' – and he did it in a direct and uncompromising way, through sending out a message of warning to anyone who thought they could lead a coup against him. He mobilized the media to dissuade anyone from such attempts at seizing power for fear of the consequences. Napoleon always maintained a tight censorship of the press – not least for military security – and the number of newspapers in Paris was reduced to a handful by 1811; many of the articles were written by the Emperor himself.

7. **Election** – to select by voting, to be appointed as a result; a plebiscite or referendum as a way of voting on a simple one-way decision; the power gained by a leader as a result of a popular election.

Napoleon was to use the power provided by popular election and popular acclaim to become Emperor – he was voted to this specially-invented hereditary title after a build-up of his celebrity status in 1804. This increase in power followed the negotiations with the Catholic Church resulting in the Concordat, the Treaty of Amiens and a high-profile crack-down on assassination attempts. He was winning hearts among Frenchmen, however contrived this may have been on his part. He appeared to be popular, even though behind the scenes he was rooting out opponents and becoming more of a dictator. By demonstrating his popularity amongst the population he silenced opposition to his concentration of power; a perfect example of the turn from populism to tyranny. In the plebiscite establishing the Empire, he was the only candidate and garnered three and a half million 'yes' votes against a mere 2,500 'no' votes. But he still felt the need to invent thousands of phony votes from the army, as he wanted to show resounding support from the half a million soldiers massed on the Normandy cliffs ready to invade England – and they hadn't shown the kind of enthusiasm he wanted.

This was planned as the election to end all elections: the massive showy coronation enthused those needing inspiration and encouraged them to revel in *la Gloire* and *l'Honneur*, desperately wanted after the disruption of 15 years of revolution, war and chaos. The Empire promised security and stability, though in the event it lasted for just another two years before war broke out again.

8. **Inheritance** – A means to pass property or titles to the next generation, on the basis that these are characteristics analogous to hereditary physical and personal traits. It deals with the problem of succession by reference to the person rather than the role or the task; and is thus counter to meritocracy; but is well founded in the customs and practices of most societies. It extends to the concept of receiving a benefit from predecessors, and the desire to provide an inheritance to others; to care for one's own people in the face of mortality.

Napoleon's power base lacked that which he resented in others, and wanted most of all for himself: the legitimacy of power by hereditary right. He had created an empire, placed himself at its pinnacle; had been anointed by the Pope; had married the daughter of Europe's oldest royal family; yet he craved inherited legitimacy, to found a dynasty that his successors could inherit and continue a Napoleonic legacy.

In this he failed (discounting the inglorious accession of Napoleon III and the Second Empire); but his impact on Europe was as great as any leader: we are all his inheritors.

A CHRONOLOGY OF NAPOLEON'S CAREER

Napoleon Bonaparte (a young artillery officer from Corsica, of Italian descent) rose rapidly through the ranks to become a General at the age of 26. As we suggest above, his story is that of an exercise in power – in various forms which changed as his career progressed.

He came from a modest Corsican family with some antique links to nobility, freedom fighters against Genoese occupation and later reconciled to French colonialism. Thanks to their ability to win the **patronage** of the newly installed Governor, he was able as a young man to win a place at Brienne, a prestigious military academy on the mainland. This form of power – patronage and reward – was to characterize Napoleon's future leadership style and became one of his methods for attracting and retaining support and building his power base – including through his family members.

Graduating with honours as an artillery officer, he identified with the egalitarian ideas of the French Revolution and benefited from vacancies created by the exile and execution of so many aristocratic officers. He was thus able to quickly shine in a series of stunning victories. But this was not just the absence of competition; his promotion from captain to brigadier-general in just four months after the Siege of Toulon in 1793 was obviously gained through his own **merit**. His brilliance in battle and logistics was to increase his credibility in his subsequent bid for political power in France. But although an outstanding general, he was never seen as a military dictator. Military ability and excellence in the field was a tool, rather than an end in itself.

Napoleon continued to lead from the front, his undoubted **charisma** giving him the edge over other up-and-coming military leaders in the Italian Wars – especially shown by acts of inspirational bravado at the battles for bridges at Arcola and Lodi. His legend was beginning to spread, encouraged by his own efforts at self-aggrandizement and publicity through constant memoranda, essay writing and lobbying the press.

The Italian Wars were followed by adventures further afield; he led the largest ever invasion fleet to Egypt, following a dream to march onto India and attack England in her colonies. But Napoleon's Egyptian campaign began to run out of steam when his army was trapped by Nelson's fleet, sinking his ships at the mouth of the Nile. He abandoned his army, returned to France, overthrew the government and had himself appointed First Consul by a **seizure** of power. The coup known as Brumaire brought to an end the much-criticized Directory, and was just the latest in a series of coups and collapses, from the fall of the Bastille, bread riots, the Girondins and the Jacobins, the execution of the King and Queen, and the rise and fall of Robespierre.

Somewhat at odds with his meritocratic ideals, Napoleon turned to his family to fill key roles, with which he persisted in spite of their obvious lack of competence and commitment. He was especially disappointed with his marriage to Josephine, who didn't live up to his expectations of obedience and fidelity. He became cold and defensive in personal relations, obsessed with political ambition and what might now be recognized as workaholism.

The rapidly-growing legend of Napoleon as statesman as well as general soon outshone his apparent opportunism, although his power base increasingly depended on **manipulation**. Napoleon needed to negotiate with internal and external parties to get his way, especially as he lacked the legitimacy of the monarchy overthrown by the Revolution, and faced continual opposition from the crowned heads of Europe. At best they became hesitant and temporary allies, at worst outright enemies. He found it very difficult to work in partnership with anyone, becoming increasingly individualistic and less and less of a team player. An example of his manipulative approach to power at this time may be seen in his relationship with the Papacy. The Concordat with Pope Pius VII was negotiated by Napoleon against internal advice. He wanted to acknowledge the Catholicism of most of the population and to separate this from any attachment to the old royal family. But a key reform of the Revolution had been sale of church lands, and returning these to the church would have been wildly unpopular with the bourgeoisie and larger landowners. The Concordat was a diplomatic victory, though Napoleon was later to imprison the Pope in Savoy, even though he had needed him at his coronation as Emperor.

As First Consul, Napoleon was the constitutional leader in France, but he was concerned with the vulnerability of his position in the face of continuing opposition – within his group of advisers, among his generals and especially coming from the disenfranchised former aristocracy of France. He managed the media and sources of information, and kept those around him in check by an elaborate system of patronage and reward – and the use of spies. When this was not enough, he began to exercise power through **fear,** especially after a series of assassination attempts. To show who was in charge, potential opponents were dealt with harshly – especially in the case of the duc d'Enghien, accused of involvement in a plot to replace Napoleon, tried on fabricated evidence, and executed *pour décourager les autres*. Napoleon later commented that the execution of d'Enghien was a grave political mistake since it alienated him from the other European Courts, all populated by aristocrats like d'Enghien.

Napoleon always believed that his leadership needed to become strengthened and institutionalized to build his legitimacy amongst his peers in Europe. He always felt vulnerable as a parvenu. The act of crowning himself Emperor was the result, he maintained, of popular **election,** by more than three million Frenchmen. Ironically, he wanted to become the monarch that his espoused Revolution had aimed to destroy.

The Napoleonic legend ultimately lost its shine with his military defeats – including the spectacular retreat from Moscow – and frustrating exile. But he never lost his appeal for the French, who still admire *la Gloire*, *l'honneur*, and the cult of Napoleon as his legacy continues – although his hope to create a dynasty based on **inheritance** was short-lived. On his defeat and exile in 1814, his greatest disappointment was not the loss of his throne, but the failure of his advisers and family to support his queen Marie-Louise as Regent and the King of Rome as his heir, and the rapid re-installation of the Bourbons – as if the Napoleonic era had counted for nothing.

The **outline** of Napoleon's life is well-known, especially as a series of dramatic military achievements. He was born (15 August 1769) in Ajaccio, Corsica, and began studying at the royal military academy in France in 1779, through a stroke of luck in finding a local patron and winning his support. Having moved to France, enrolled in the military school, he graduated in 1785 with the rank of second lieutenant in the artillery. Then stationed in Valence, he watched history being made on 14 July 1789 as the Paris mob stormed the Bastille. A precedent of French people being led by a sudden seizure of power was being made. Three years later, while in Paris with his regiment, Napoleon witnessed an attack on the Tuileries Palace and the dethroning and guillotining of the French King, Louis XVI. Convinced that his future lay with the French after his training in France and enthusiasm for the Revolution, and now accused of being too pro-French, Napoleon and his family were forced to flee from their home in Corsica. By the end of 1793, Napoleon was very much part of the post-revolutionary French establishment, and was manipulating his continued accumulation of power. For courage in battle at Toulon, he was promoted to brigadier-general, at a time when aristocratic army officers were in hiding or in exile or had been executed, and able young soldier officers were rapidly shooting up the ranks – especially those of genuine military merit and charisma such as Napoleon.

In revolutions it is easy to suddenly be on the wrong side, and this is what happened to Napoleon in August 1794; he was imprisoned under suspicion of being a Jacobin and a supporter of Robespierre. But a year later he was released and promoted to General of the Army of the West. By October 1795 in a rapid about-turn in his fortunes he was assigned the task of suppressing civil strife and rebellion against the Republic. He commanded the decisive shooting of 200 rebels and was given command of the Army of the Interior. He was rapidly learning how to go about managing an effective power base.

After a succession of unsatisfactory romances, when at the home of Paul-Francois Barras, a Directory member, Napoleon met Rose de Beauharnais. With Barras' help, he was promoted to Commander of the Army of the Interior and given command of the French Army in Italy. Flushed with success, excitement and conviction of his future destiny, Napoleon married his Josephine (the name he always gave her) and days later in March 1796 the Italian campaign against Austria began.

Winning the Battle of Lodi two months later, he capped this with the Battles of Arcola and Rivoli, drawing up the Treaty of Campo-Formio with Austria in late 1797.

Returning to Paris a hero, Napoleon continued to strengthen his military and political position, and was sufficiently confident to undertake an ambitious, long-distance campaign in Egypt, accompanied by an army of cultural experts as well as tens of thousands of soldiers. The fall of Alexandria was closely followed by Napoleon's success at the Battle of the Pyramids against the Mamelukes, and then he captured Cairo. Frustrated to be away from Josephine and hearing rumours of her infidelity, a colder and sterner side of his nature began to appear, together with an ambition fired by the experience of running an entire country – albeit by military occupation.

Napoleon's run of success started to falter: under the command of Admiral Nelson, a British squadron destroyed the French fleet at the Battle of Aboukir, leaving Napoleon's armies stranded in Egypt. Things went from bad to worse a year later when, receiving news of political turmoil and unrest in France, Napoleon returned to Paris, forced to leave his troops behind. With the help of his brother Lucien and following a partly-botched coup d'état during a time of almost complete political collapse, Napoleon seized power and eventually became First Consul of the new French government, setting up a household in the Tuileries Palace for himself and Josephine at the start of the new century.

Napoleon was now the ruler of France in more ways than one, especially when a popular vote elected him Life Consul. With continuing instability around the French borders and ongoing opposition to the Revolution from throughout Europe, Napoleon led a new army across the Alps in the Second Italian Campaign. Winning the Battle of Marengo against Austria, he signed a peace treaty at Luneville in February 1800. Then confronting His Holiness the Pope, in July 1801 Napoleon concluded the Concordat between France and Rome, ending the schism between the French government and the Catholic Church. Less than a year later he was to sign the short-lived Treaty of Amiens with Britain. In a brief period of calm and peace, Napoleon worked on reforming his chaotic adopted country – financially, economically, legally and educationally – soon further consolidating his strong political position in the face of declining opposition and continued dislike of the Bourbons in France. Ruling increasingly through manipulation and political connivance, he was able to maintain what he saw as the continuation of the Revolution's goals – but for how long?

Concerned with the fragility of the new order in France and his own mortality after a scary assassination attempt, Napoleon led a fierce crackdown on suspected political opponents. Understandably he and many others wanted a clear process to manage the succession, avoiding a return to the chaotic series of ineffective attempts at government that Napoleon had so decisively resolved in the Brumaire coup d'état. But strangely he saw the only solution to be hereditary succession by his own dynasty – ironically to replace the Bourbons. In August 1802 a new constitution was adopted, making Napoleon First Consul for Life, building up to his proclamation as Emperor in May 1804, again ratified by popular election. Following his coronation in December in Notre-Dame Cathedral, Napoleon was also crowned King of Italy in Milan.

Despite his accumulation of power and increasing military strength in mainland Europe, Napoleon was constantly thwarted by England, and with his reversal at sea at the Battle of Trafalgar (another naval defeat of France by a British fleet under the command of Admiral Nelson), Napoleon turned his attention towards attacking Austria and Russia. With victory at the Battles of Austerlitz and Friedland, Napoleon consolidated his power base by using his own form of nepotistic patronage – by appointing his numerous family members to kingdoms across Europe, naming his brother Joseph as King of Naples. Making peace with Tsar Alexander I at Tilsit, Napoleon created the Grand Duchy of Warsaw to replace the truncated Poland, to be overseen by France.

Still surrounded on all the borders of France by pro-Bourbon and anti-revolutionary opposition, by late 1807 Napoleon led the French occupation of Portugal, and sent French marshal Joachim Murat to lead an army in Spain. After an unsuccessful Spanish revolt against the French army, by mid-1808 Napoleon had named his brother Joseph, King of Spain, and Murat, King of Naples.

Yet he continued to be concerned with the creation and longevity of his own dynasty, so in December 1809 Napoleon reluctantly divorced Josephine, marrying Marie-Louise, Archduchess of Austria, a few months later. Previously without a legitimate son and heir, great rejoicing followed the birth, in March 1811, of Napoleon's son, referred to as the 'King of Rome' – his attempt at creating a lasting inherited line. This alliance was also intended to cement a relationship with his new father-in-law, Emperor Francis I of Austria, but this attempt at building peace in Europe was not to flourish as Napoleon intended.

Feeling cornered on all fronts and seeing no alternative, Napoleon made the ill-fated decision to start a campaign to invade Russia and capture Moscow. Setting off in June 1812, three months later the Grand Army entered Moscow to find the city abandoned and set on fire by the inhabitants; retreating in the midst of a frigid winter, the army suffered devastating losses and Napoleon returned to Paris in December 1812 with a small fraction of his vast army straggling far behind. From then on, Napoleon's military prowess – one of the most fundamental aspects of his power base – was under sustained attack, his enemies encouraged and inspired by the enormity of the defeat in Russia. In March 1813 even the apparently vacillating Frederick William of Prussia declared war on France; the French forces fell to Spain in the Battle of Vitoria; by January 1814 anti-French coalition armies entered France; and Paris was captured by combined enemy forces in March. Tired of war, the Parisians put up no resistance and Prime Minister Talleyrand stayed back to negotiate a transfer of power to the Bourbons. Despite a network of supporters and his widespread and elaborate system of patronage, Napoleon was alone.

The Senate then proclaimed the end of the Empire. Napoleon's wife and son fled from Paris, the Emperor abdicated his rule and, despite his plea that his son as Heir and wife as Regent should succeed him, Louis XVIII, a Bourbon, was restored to the French throne. Napoleon was exiled to the island of Elba, whilst his wife and son took refuge in Vienna with her father, the Emperor of Austria, one of the first to desert Napoleon when his star was no longer in the ascendant.

But this was not the end of the story. Escaping Elba in March 1815, Napoleon returned to the South of France, rallied the French army in a great show of personal charisma and opportunism, and forced Louis XVIII to flee from Paris. Napoleon moved back into the Tuileries as if nothing had happened, took control, and began the 'Hundred Days' campaign. Following a series of almost daily battles, his army was finally defeated at the Battle of Waterloo on 18 June 1815 by the British and Prussians, led by Wellington and Blucher. Napoleon was forced to abdicate for the second time, and exiled to the much more distant and inhospitable island of St Helena, where he languished in exile until his death on 5 May 1821. The long hoped-for inheritance of his son never happened, and this was one of his greatest disappointments.

PATRONAGE

The Scholarship, 1776–78 : the first great opportunity — and setting up obligations for dispensing patronage in the future

For Napoleon, the importance of making contacts was instilled by his father Carlo Bonaparte in Corsica. The Corsican clan system represented 'an astute exploitation of opportunities'.

Dwyer, 2007, pp515–6

If only Father were here now to see this!

Napoleon to his older brother Joseph, at his coronation as Emperor, 1804

Napoleon rewarded all his brothers but they 'requited his favour with incompetence, defiance and treachery'.

McLynn, 1998, p663

In the ... complicated and hard-hitting school of Corsican politics ... Napoleon acquired his political apprenticeship ... in a society based on the clan, status was assessed by the solidarity of the family, and feuds were settled by private vengeance – the Corsican vendetta.

Markham, 1963, p16

Napoleon made political appointments to please his supplicants ... 'he must maintain a balance between the clans and root his power in all

the self-interests. He has no illusions … he must give, that is what is
expected of him, and he needs to so that people remain loyal.'.

Gallo, 1997a, p252

Nothing annoyed Napoleon more … than the name given to him by his
enemies, 'the Corsican'. He did not attach much importance to his ori-
gins and lineage; he claimed to be a self-made man whose titles rested
on his sword and on the desires of the French nation … he retained to
the end of his life a sense of family loyalty and obligation which was a
markedly Corsican trait; but when he came to power 'a foreign origin
was an embarrassment which had to be hidden like bastardy'.

Markham, 1963, p15

Napoleon owed his impetus to be a leader to patronage: this is how he
made his start in his military, then political life, and how he created a
network of supporters and built his power base. This is the subject of our
first chapter: it all began in Corsica. Understanding this context is essential to understanding Napoleon. As a young man he won his first big
break through gaining a place at a prestigious military school in France,
arranged for him by the new French Governor of Corsica, who was willing to help the Bonapartes in order to gain their support as a prominent
Corsican family. Napoleon gladly accepted this patronage and was later
to use patronage to bolster his own power base, especially promoting his
close family and their relations.

Corsica is a small Mediterranean island with Italian antecedents. The
strength of the community, still largely apparent in this region, is in
contrast with the more individualistic, independent and less clannish
northern Europeans. Status and respect is everything. Shame cannot be
tolerated; loss of face must be avenged, and loyalty is a matter of honour
as well as reward. Systems of patronage, based on family and community ties, are an essential part of the culture.

This is where Napoleon grew up. The Bonapartes were a prominent
local family with obligations and responsibilities to the community, and
long-established loyalties and enmities. These pressures dominated the
first decade of Napoleon's life, and inevitably influenced his attitudes in
his formative years.

Napoleon's father was fashionable and landed. The Bonaparte family could be traced back 200 years to Tuscany, and claimed traces of

nobility when necessary. His mother was a girl from a military family. Marrying for love was popular in the unsophisticated, small rustic island of 130,000 people – not for them the strategic dynastic marriages of the leading families of Paris.

From the start, Carlo and Letizia Bonaparte encouraged their active and wayward second son to be ambitious – and this was a time of excitement and revolt in Corsica. A nationalist rebellion against the Genoese colonists, with an inspirational and heroic claim for independence, thrilled and inspired the Bonaparte couple. Indeed, the young Napoleon, whilst still in the womb, was campaigning in the mountains near Ajaccio. He was named after a favourite uncle of Letizia who had fought the French and who had died shortly before her second son's birth.

Napoleon was born French, but only just. In the early 1760s, the rebel leader Paoli, a devoted anti-colonial guerrilla fighter, had driven the hated Genoese out of much of Corsica and was trying to lead the island to independence. Strongly supported by the Bonapartes who shared Paoli's disgust with the way Corsicans were abused by their occupiers, Paoli had plans to enforce law and order and build roads and schools. Napoleon was born in the ferment of active hatred of a colonial oppressor who treated Corsicans as vassals, where aristocratic Genoese were favoured for advancement, and where rebel fighters fought in the hills, harried by local bandits as well as their political enemies. They had no uniforms, few weapons and lived off the land. They survived because they knew the terrain better than anyone else. Napoleon stayed true to much of this native Corsican tradition – of being anti-feudal, anti-colonial, anti-aristocratic, fiercely independent and unfazed by difficult geographical terrain and conditions. Like Paoli, Napoleon was to be dedicated to education, a keen reader of the classics and vastly energetic in the cause to which he was committed.

Napoleon was born French and not Italian because just months before his birth, the Genoese decided to sell Corsica to France. The French, arriving to take possession of their new acquisition, faced the fiery, loud, gun-toting and determined Corsican rebels, who rapidly switched to attacking a new enemy. After some successes against their new occupiers, Paoli, the Bonapartes and their followers (including the infant Joseph and the embryonic Napoleon) were hopelessly outnumbered and forced to capitulate. Paoli and 300 close supporters went into exile in England rather than face a new form of colonial oppression.

But the practical and opportunistic Carlo Bonaparte decided to stay in Ajaccio and bring up his growing family. They lived in a big inherited house, with other generations of the family and more distant relatives living on the other floors. Letizia went to Mass every morning, even when she had started to go into labour with Napoleon, who was born on the feast of the Virgin – 15 August 1769. The Bonapartes lived off the produce of their estates – 'the Bonapartes never paid for bread, wine and oil' (Cronin, 1971: 18–19); there was no coinage, only barter, and the land and what it could produce was the basis of all wealth. There was little incentive to amass capital, and a happy family life and high standing in the community was what mattered. Napoleon was to learn a lot from this: you looked after your relatives as they looked after you; religion was very powerful; land is the fundamental form of wealth; status in the community was of extreme importance; having a happy family life was highly desirable. From his father's stories he learned of the power of a close-knit group of rebels defending their own patch, drawing on their experience at hunting: birds, animals or enemy soldiers.

Carlo recognized the new dispensation of power, and pragmatically ingratiated himself with the French as they became more established on Corsica. He particularly made the effort to meet the new French governor of the island, the comte de Marbeuf, who arrived in the mid-1770s. Marbeuf was to play a key role as Napoleon's godfather – in more ways than one. He was his sponsor and patron, but also acted as a 'godfather' amidst the factions and infighting on the island. Marbeuf was immediately attracted to Napoleon's parents amongst his constituents on Corsica. They were a handsome pair – Letitzia had striking beauty and character, Carlo was charming, cultured and well-educated if rather weak and extravagant – and they were good company for the older, childless and lonely Marbeuf, on his own in Corsica representing the French overlords, and still facing some hostility.

Carlo's co-operation with the French helped to assert the family's prestige in the community. After a lengthy application process, also helped by Marbeuf, Carlo was elevated to the French nobility on Corsica, and the Bonapartes emerged as one of the leading families of Ajaccio. As Napoleon recalled, 'we thought ourselves as good as the Bourbons: in the island we really were' (Markham, 1963: 17).

But Napoleon's mother Letitzia never stopped reminding him that the Bonapartes had been poor, and might at any moment go back to being poor; in adversity they should put on a brave show, and bear discomfort. As young aristocrats of limited means, Napoleon and his older brother Joseph were entitled to be educated for free by the French state – and again the Bonapartes needed the intervention of the helpful Marbeuf to prove their aristocratic connections.

Luckily for Napoleon, the clannish and old-fashioned nature of planning children's careers followed the tradition in Corsica that the eldest son went into the Church, and the second son to the army – otherwise Napoleon might have made a dubious and frustrated member of the clergy.

Marbeuf helped the eldest son Joseph into training for the priesthood, and also enabled the young Napoleon to enter one of the most prestigious military schools in France. The arrangement suited Marbeuf too. With no children of his own, he was happy to mentor the young Bonaparte children, whilst also fulfilling what he saw as a series of diplomatic obligations. With Corsica newly part of France, Marbeuf had been told by the Minister of Foreign Affairs to 'make yourself loved by the Corsicans, and neglect nothing to make them love France' (Cronin, 1971: 25).

Marbeuf's remit included the administration of justice, in the course of which he had to adapt to the strong moral standards that placed loyalty to family and personal honour above statute and rule. He soon became accustomed to Corsican ways, of vendettas, an obsession with violent death, of the importance of love, honour, justice and fair play. As Napoleon was later to remark, 'a Corsican would never think of abandoning even his tenth cousin' (Markham, 1963: 16). This attitude is in stark contrast with the looser family connections in northern Europe, and the modern rationalism that accompanied the Revolution. It might help to explain the rather naïve trust that Napoleon placed in 'family' – such as his belief that marrying Marie-Louise, daughter of the Emperor of Austria, would be enough to cement a political and military alliance. It counted for little when Napoleon really needed it.

For Napoleon, life changed dramatically in December 1778 when, blessed by the Father Superior, this confident 9-year-old set off for the military academy of Brienne, one of twelve royal schools for the sons of nobles founded in 1776 by St Germain, Louis XVI's Minister of War. He was bullied for his foreign accent and poverty, defending himself as a persecuted Corsican patriot, and he must have suffered the usual anxieties of a child sent away to school: some have suggested that he harboured a subconscious jealousy of his mother's close friendship with Marbeuf. Especially after the death of his father, Napoleon must have wondered about his patron's hidden motives.

Reflections on leadership and power

- Napoleon was brought up to be a leader – especially to respond to family obligations.

- His family background included rebels and fighters and had a tradition of independence and hating colonialism – Napoleon was expected to continue this.

- Napoleon was talented, intelligent, passionate, capable of inspiring others but could be petty and vindictive – which is seen as typical of Corsican politics and society.

- But France was taking over Corsica – the Bonapartes opportunistically stayed rather than following Paoli into exile, and then rose to aristocratic status helped by the French Governor Marbeuf.

- Marbeuf's support of the Bonaparte children gave Napoleon his start in life, but this patronage through his parents put him under an obligation to succeed.

- Patronage and reward (and opportunism) helped Napoleon to join the leadership track.

- Patronage as a way of gaining support was used by Napoleon all his life.

- The strong influence of Corsican community culture was prominent in Napoleon's background – supporting the family, avoiding shame, seeking revenge/honour when wronged, valuing independence, living off the land, sharing any wealth.

- Patronage was being used to develop a network of supporters – by Paoli, by Carlo Bonaparte, and then by Napoleon himself.

- In this context, potential leaders receive patronage to become leaders, and then are expected to give it to others.

Napoleon's parents used the networking and relationship-oriented ways of operating in Corsica to good effect. Napoleon's family, with their aristocratic status on the island, encouraged their sons (and daughters) to seek high positions in society. When France took over Corsica and officially recognized the Bonapartes, they were looked up to – especially when they curried favour with the French Governor. They were indeed lucky that Governor Marbeuf was childless and willing to support the many Bonaparte children. Marbeuf's generosity in being a patron to the young Napoleon put the latter under an obligation to succeed and pay back his benefactor, living up to his expectations.

Patronage and reward was the way that Napoleon first joined the leadership track – and it became a cultural norm which he had to recognize all his life. The pressure of Corsican culture was strong from the start; help is provided by patrons, then the recipient of patronage gives help back to the patrons and their current and future supporters. Patronage and reward became the cornerstone of Napoleon's early obsession with leadership, pushing him to fulfil the expectations of his benefactor.

Patronage comes with strings attached; already Napoleon was under pressure to succeed, to meet the expectations of his well-to-do patron. He also increasingly felt an obligation to support his mother and her seven children, especially as older brother Joseph was much less ambitious and responsible.

Napoleon was to remember the vital role of Marbeuf in giving him a start in life, and recognized the sense of obligation it laid upon him. Along with his rising power and influence came opportunities for ever more lavish patronage.

The Bonapartes' friendship with Marbeuf made for an easier choice between supporting Corsican independence and welcoming the coming French occupation (though it was to lead to their eventual exile from their homeland). Napoleon never regretted throwing in his lot with the French and later, in supporting the Revolution rather than the aristocracy, he backed another winner.

When in power himself Napoleon too often focused patronage on his siblings, appointing them to positions of power and wealth. He gained little by doing so: they were already on his side, and were mostly ill-suited to the roles. Thus he used these most prominent opportunities for patronage to reward his family, rather than to extend the network of obligation and loyalty around him.

But this is understandable. Napoleon wanted to ensure that his siblings and their supporters would owe allegiance to him, and at the same time to avoid setting up potential rivals to his own position. But as he enriched his followers, they became more concerned to protect their gains, and less willing to embark on risky military escapades or radical political reforms. And like any leader, as his power began to wane, Napoleon could offer less to his followers, so the most powerful amongst them shifted allegiance to his up-and-coming successors.

Patronage is crucial to the influence wielded by any political or corporate leader: in a complex enterprise most of the work is done by people the leader can trust. Trust and loyalty are substantially underpinned by obligation and gratitude, which are bought by patronage.

The advantage of the power of patronage is that it can quickly build mutual support and a network of acolytes, and for Napoleon it was culturally obligatory. But the downside can be an expectation of rewards purely on the basis of family connections and long-term service – and those receiving the rewards increasingly wanted to preserve their wealth and enjoy their new status and comfort. So patronage and reward power can foster a sense of entitlement and greed, and taking the patron for granted.

Patronage rests on an assumption that wisdom is a possession of those with power – that wisdom and power are united in the same person. Patronage is fundamental to feudalism, the distribution of resources by which wealth is created, which is seen as legitimately derived from a central authority with wisdom and power. To obtain access to resources, there is a need to obtain a patron, who controls these resources. Throughout the Renaissance, artists relied on patronage. Wealthy people would patronize them and give them work. Patrons expected that those they patronized would flatter them, owe them a debt of obligation, and do their best work in their name. This concept of obligation is funda-mental to the system of patronage, and the processes of patronage are seen as natural and inevitable. Showing loyalty to a patron is essential in the point of view of a ruler; rulers recognize a need to create a fertile social network of obligation to feed and sustain their regimes.

Patronage as the natural order of things goes back to classical times, and was espoused by Xenophon in his historical novel *Cyropaedia*, in which he analysed the rule of Cyrus the Great of Persia. In this 'master-class' in the use of patronage, Xenophon explains how Cyrus would give gifts and honours of status without any overt contract. He could assume that the recipients of patronage would give their loyalty, at least to some extent, although this dependency on patronage does not entirely explain the long-term obligations then seen as an impor-tant part of maintaining a system. Patronage was used to reinforce this dependency, and worked much more effectively than depending only on short-term transactions.

A cultural system of beliefs as well as pragmatic social contracts came together with patronage to create feudal societies. In the era of the French Revolution and Napoleon, these were taken over by other ideologies which were supplemented but not replaced by a meritocracy, but the contemporary relevance of patronage continued then and now.

In modern examples, we can see the political leader who declares his or her intention not to run for office any more, and how immediately his or her potential to hold out the gift of patronage and support dries up.

In the professions, there can be two possibilities for bringing on the next generation. Young people are supported through being selected by objective criteria; or leading professionals select and support the young people they deem most worthy to receive their organization's patronage, based on their experience, knowledge and judgement. The former approach removes the power of patronage from individual professionals – the young person worth supporting is chosen by a committee, which has agreed to pre-determined bureaucratic processes and procedures, referring to ostensibly meritocratic neutrality. Arguably, this system leads to a bland and unadventurous approach and little opportunity to adapt to changing circumstances. By contrast, the approach favouring patronage gives resources to a proven expert and along with this the freedom to develop new and creative ideas.

Advocates of the latter, feudal-like system argue that it preserves high quality because the bureaucratic alternative inevitably leads to mediocrity, as candidates play the system of emphasizing the favoured criteria and structuring their approach accordingly. Should there be open advertisements for jobs whereby candidates are mechanically selected by key words, or appointment made by internal and external experts? There is always the feeling that patronage is associated with nepotism and other forms of corruption, as critics of this system point out. But within the ideology of patronage, the open and transparent giving and receiving of patronage is accepted; it depends on the dominant ideology of the regime.

As we will see in this book, Napoleon squandered his patronage on his family members. He didn't have to give favours to his family to buy their loyalty, but the fact that he did so was the most powerful demonstration that he was still living in a society dominated by a clan-based approach to patronage, rather than seeing a systemic understanding of the value of patronage. A more sophisticated appreciation of patronage may have led him to distribute favours among those whose loyalty and participation was more reliable and competent. Napoleon's patronage was wasted on his family as they were either loyal or disloyal, depending on their inclinations, and they mostly used his patronage to be independent of him. In the feudal system of old, a king would give patronage, and then take it back if the person receiving it turned out to be undeserving; Napoleon did not feel able to do this. His ability to dispense patronage effectively was undermined by his lack of legitimacy and his dependence on winning battles and other short-term needs, and as we have seen, he did not always choose the recipients of his patronage as wisely and effectively as he could have done.

Questions on leadership and power

Why do you want to be a leader? Is it at least partly to fulfil expectations and reward a patron? And to use patronage yourself to gain the support of those around you?

- Did you use patronage to get to your position of power?
- What was the role of your family in your leadership progression? Encouragement or discouragement?
- Have you or your patrons been principled or opportunistic in achieving a leadership role?
- Was the patronage you received with or without obligation?
- Do you now behave in a way similar to those who were your patrons in the past, by being a patron of others?
- Have you deliberately used patronage to build up a network of supporters?
- Do you think you are using your patronage wisely – are you bestowing your patronage on the right people?
- How are you influenced by the culture of your homeland or where you were brought up in your relationships?

MERIT

The Siege of Toulon, 1793: the beginnings of a new meritocratic system, but how long would it last?

To the very last, he [Napoleon] had a kind of idea; that, namely, of 'la carriere ouverte aux talents': a career open to talents, the tools to him that can handle them.

Carlyle, 1960, p98

There is only one possible plan – Bonaparte's.

His superior, 1793

Words fail me to describe Bonaparte's merits. He has plenty of knowledge, and as much intelligence and courage: and that is no more than a first sketch of the virtues of a most rare officer.

Reported by a superior to the Minister of War, 1794

I promised you brilliant successes, and, as you see, I have kept my word.

Napoleon to the Minister of War, 1794

Always remember three things: concentration of one's forces, constant activity, and firm resolve to perish with glory ... these are the ... principles of military art, which have always made Fortune favourable in all my operations.

Napoleon

All the business of war... is to endeavour to find out what you don't know from what you do; that's what I call 'guessing what was at the other side of the hill'.

Wellington, 1812

An army marches on its stomach.

Napoleon

Napoleon in Paris had no connections – only his ability – so he dawdled there trying to get a better posting. Saliceti helped him get the Toulon opportunity, then he ran into Barras who was to help him make other contacts, including meeting Josephine. It was hard for Napoleon in France compared with when he was at home in Corsica.

Dwyer, 2007, pp515–6

Napoleon's performance at the Siege of Toulon is an example of a show of exceptional talent in the field. He had joined the French army in 1785, as an artillery officer, but after the Siege of Toulon he became 'the man of the moment'; it put him on the map towards becoming a successful general, and then eventually to entering politics. Through a display of merit, Napoleon – who had thrown in his lot with the winning side – was seen as an outstanding soldier, helping him to gain credibility in the lead up to seizing power. The Siege of Toulon, in December 1793, was the opportunity he needed to shine. Napoleon had a chance to prove his worth as a military man when he was still very young, and this became the first stepping stone to fame and glory. Without it, he would have lacked the opportunity to climb to greater things. How he did it is the focus of this chapter.

In 1793, Toulon, with a population of 28,000, was a dangerous pro-Royalist rebel city. It was the second most important naval base in France, but had allowed the entry of British and Spanish fleets, who were taking the opportunity to attack French merchantmen, blockade French ports and take over French colonies. Part of the city was inviting the foreigners as a counter-revolutionary gesture, and other parts were fighting them.

The commander of the anti-rebel French forces and part of the anti-rebel Montagnard faction was General Carteaux, who knew nothing of siege warfare, but was about to find himself the lucky commander of someone who did. Napoleon, then only 24, was the only artillery captain on the spot able to plan and launch operations. He had just been part of a unit stopping the rebels of Marseilles from joining the rebels of Lyon. Everywhere the pro-revolutionary forces were short of artillery, in both manpower and guns, so Napoleon was in demand and rapidly gaining experience. The Bonaparte family, forced into exile from Corsica by a momentarily successful independence movement opposing their support of the French, was living in Marseilles during this critical phase of the revolutionary war.

In the first two days of the Siege of Toulon the previous artillery commander, Dommartin, had been wounded. With Napoleon available to replace him, Saliceti – the Deputy in the Committee of Public Safety responsible for this theatre of war – explained, 'chance has helped us well; we have retained Captain Bonaparte, an experienced officer, who was on his way to the Army of Italy, and ordered him to replace Dommartin' (Markham, 1963: 25). Saliceti was particularly on the lookout for fellow Corsicans, attempting to build a force that might in the future be capable of securing the island of Corsica for the Revolution. He was therefore on the lookout for talent, sending most of them to join the army in Italy.

Napoleon, appointed temporarily in September 1793 and given considerable autonomy, first of all identified a strategic position overlooking the western promontory of Toulon between the inner and outer harbours. The position was controlled by a fortress occupied by British marines. This was the first encounter between Napoleon and British sea power, so he was up against a strong enemy from the start. If this position could be captured, he could render both of these harbours untenable to foreign shipping. But he had too few guns and men to take the fort, so he laid siege and set about gathering the resources for an attack.

When Napoleon's superior General Carteaux took him to inspect the available artillery, the young man was shocked to see that the French anti-rebel forces had only two 24-pounders and two 16-pounder guns. Carteaux was under the belief that these guns could hit the British ships three miles away out to sea. He had no idea that they had a range of less than a mile – from these emplacements the shot would hardly hit the coastline. Napoleon suggested making a sighting round; this was embarrassing, as Carteaux did not know what a sighting round was (it is a single shot fired to see how far it will reach). On further tactful explanation from his young artillery officer, Carteaux blamed the Marseilles suppliers for sending poor-quality gunpowder.

Nevertheless Napoleon thought these guns could still do some damage. He immediately suggested using the kitchen of a nearby farmhouse and, with brass bellows, set about making red-hot shot to fire incendiary rounds at the ships. In spite of an obviously incompetent commander, Napoleon realized he had an opportunity here. Shocked and disgusted by the civil war and unwilling to fire on Frenchmen, he took the war to the English.

Seeing that he seemed to know what he was doing, Carteaux gave
Napoleon a free reign with the artillery, and sought his advice on a range
of military matters. Napoleon requisitioned extra guns from Antibes and
Monaco, brought oxen from Montpellier, and hired brigades of wagon
drivers with 100,000 sacks of earth from Marseilles to build parapets to
augment his defences. He built an arsenal of 80 forges, a workshop for
repairing muskets, and dug in his guns on the sea edge where they were
better placed to pound the British fleet. Four days later a British officer in
the fleet noted that 'our gunboats suffered considerably ... 70 men killed
or wounded ... Lord Hood became anxious about the shipping' (Cronin,
1971: 87). But it was not without cost, and Carteaux, threatened by this
active young officer, took a critical stance, pointing to the gunners killed
in gun battles and anxious that the outcome was still uncertain.

By October 1793, Napoleon's zeal and efficiency had been recognized
and he was promoted to Major. This gave him more authority, and he
successfully lobbied for more resources. From just a handful of men and
guns when he arrived, Napoleon built up the artillery force at Toulon
to a total of 64 officers, 1,600 men and 194 guns or mortars. Carteaux,
still not persuaded that the artillery could break the siege and unsettled
by occasional losses, was eventually removed from his command, but his
successor was no better and short-lived. Finally, the likeable and competent Dugommier, a former sugar-planter (appointed at a time when
aristocratic officers had emigrated or been killed in the Revolution), was
given the command and Napoleon put forward his plan to seize the
high ground south of the port to be able to bombard the British fleet.
Dugommier agreed, and Napoleon launched an artillery duel with the
invading forces and the British ships for 48 hours. It was an intense
action in the course of which he developed close relationships with fellow officers, some of whom, such as Junot and Marmont, eventually
became his generals and marshals. During this battle Napoleon developed a survival trick that he was to use frequently: resting occasionally
for short periods lying on the ground wrapped in a cloak.

Napoleon was determined and persistent as well as proactive. Despite
hesitation from Deputy Saliceti and General Dugommier, he continued
his attack, in heavy rain. With his horse shot from under him – for the
first of many times – he kept going, and the strategically placed fort
held by the British eventually fell. In the tough hand-to-hand fighting,
Napoleon was wounded: a British sergeant's half-pike was stabbed into
the inside of his left thigh just above the knee. The field doctor didn't
like the look of it, and was going to amputate, but changed his mind.
Napoleon recovered but limped, and it left a deep scar. In dozens of
battles, this was to be the only wound he ever received, which gave him

a messianic quality in the eyes of his soldiers and reinforced their perception of him as charmed as well as brilliant.

By mid-December 1793 Admiral Hood, commanding the British fleet, had decided that the harbour was now indefensible and that the town should be evacuated of British and allied troops, leaving the remaining rebels to fend for themselves. The neighbouring forts were evacuated and Napoleon's guns were still firing as British and allied troops retreated out to sea and Lord Hood set fire to the arsenal.

Toulon was an important victory for the anti-rebel faction, expelling the combined forces of four nations from French soil and ending the rebellion in the south of France. Saliceti, who turned up when the fighting was all over, was lauded as a hero, and for Napoleon this was an important milestone. It was his first taste of real battle, and he and his troops had succeeded in driving the British from French soil. He demonstrated his ability to make quick decisions, lay plans, use judgement and act with boldness. During the siege Napoleon was promoted to acting Lieutenant-Colonel and was then appointed Brigadier-General. At only 24 years old, he had the rank and pay to start looking after his family. His mother and younger siblings were living in Marseille, refugees from the mounting civil strife in Corsica. The first thing Napoleon did was to move them away from the poverty of the city to a comfortable country house with servants.

The Deputies and Generals far away claimed much of the credit for the successful handling of the Siege of Toulon but the men on the spot recognized the contribution of Napoleon. One of the senior commanders there wrote to the Minister of War Augustin Robespierre (the brother of Maximilien) that 'an artillery officer of transcendent merit' had shown himself. Now Napoleon was to enjoy the patronage of the Robespierres, and through them to become the operational planner for the army of Italy, having prepared a memo on its future operations. He thus proved himself more than a man of action: he could analyse a complex geopolitical problem, articulate the options and persuasively argue a case.

But Napoleon was also showing himself as a trouble-maker: he didn't like the way things were being handled by his political superiors, and made his opinions known. After the siege, the revolutionary French authorities shot 200 officers and men of the pro-Royalist naval artillery in Toulon for letting in the British and other foreign invaders, and a further 200 civilians were executed for siding with the enemy. Dugommier had tried to stop the bloodshed, but had been forced to resign. Napoleon also officially objected, setting himself up as a critic as well as a useful supporter of the regime.

Reflections on leadership and power

- Napoleon was able to outshine others as an artillery officer – his area of technical specialization – at an early stage in his career.

- He benefited from the lack of competition from aristocratic officers – either guillotined or in exile, or on the wrong side.

- He was in the right place at the right time – with the right skills.

- He used his old networks, even though small in number and from a marginal colony – but luckily he had Corsican friends in high places.

- Napoleon's expertise as a specialist gave him the opportunity to prove his wider ability, and thence to quickly gain promotion in the field, which led to greater power later.

- He had then taken his first step towards leading the armies of the Republic and Empire – and he soon realized it.

- When Napoleon eventually came to power in France his wasn't a *military* dictatorship – but he was always a soldier first, and is still most commonly recognized for his brilliance in the field of battle.

The experience of Toulon gave Napoleon his first taste of power. Power creates both temporary and enduring cognitive changes that transform the way that leaders differentiate themselves from others. Power changes a leader's self-perception, in the way that Napoleon (especially after the Siege of Toulon) suddenly saw himself as a leader without limits, capable of great things. The power perceptions of the leader also impact on followers, making them feel more powerful and confident. This was a strong start to Napoleon's military career.

For three contextual reasons, Napoleon was fortunate at Toulon. First, he was in the artillery, and rising in the artillery required a good deal of technical merit, unlike many of the other departments of the army. So it was a chance to get noticed, even for a fairly poor and disadvantaged young man from the colonies. Promotion in the artillery was gained through experience and ability, and candidates were valued for their skill. It was one of the most professional branches of the armed forces, and was essential in siege warfare. Second, Napoleon benefited from a lack of competition as many military leaders had lost their lives in the Reign of Terror, and many aristocratic officers had already fled overseas into exile after the Revolution. So any active and able officer could quickly gain promotion. In any case, the artillery as a division tended to lack noble dominance and was traditionally more meritocratic. There were fewer opportunities to buy commissions here. Third, the Corsican connection worked for him again. Napoleon was appointed to command the artillery at Toulon through his relationship with a leading political figure named Saliceti, a Corsican friend of the Bonaparte family. A further stroke of luck came with the wounding and incapacitation of the existing artillery commander and the need for an immediate replacement – and Napoleon was in the right place at the right time.

Also, Napoleon was helped by incompetence all around him. As we saw, Napoleon's commanding officer at Toulon believed that his guns could hit the English ships three miles away out to sea. He had no idea that his guns had a range of less than a mile – the shot would hardly hit the coastline from where the guns were based, let alone hit the ships in the bay. Napoleon suggested that he should make a sighting round, but his commander didn't know what this meant.

Meanwhile, several regional departments of France were rising up against the government in France, then known as the Committee of Public Safety, formed of deputies with specific tasks. Much of the South and West of France were fighting against the Revolution, which had started in Paris – there were still clearly Royalist sympathies across many parts of the country. Civil war had erupted in the summer of 1793, encouraged by the Girondin faction which, expelled by the Montagnard faction, had joined forces with the counter-revolutionary Royalists.

Napoleon was undoubtedly an excellent artillery officer, and in an officer corps depleted by so many exiles, his talents stood out as especially outstanding. Napoleon thus shone at an early stage in his career, and with friends in high places and a large dose of luck was able to use this expertise to climb the ladder of promotion. This was to be the first step towards eventually leading the armies of the Republic and Empire. Being a brilliant general was always his hallmark. Napoleon was a soldier first and foremost, and was increasingly recognized for his stunning victories in the field. As his enemies said about him even at the end of his career, 'expect a defeat whenever the Emperor attacks in person. Attack and defeat his lieutenants whenever you can. Once they are beaten, assemble all your forces against Napoleon and give him no respite' (Markham, 1963: 206).

Belief in victory was helped by the meritocratic attitude which Napoleon encouraged in his soldiers, who were inspired to believe in the egalitarian view of being revolutionary citizens: 'every soldier had a field marshal's baton in his knapsack'. This was emphasized by the creation of the *Légion d'honneur* by Napoleon in 1802, especially because it was open to all ranks.

Napoleon's successes in the field of battle were impressive. Before Russia, when on a winning streak, he had fought 38 battles, winning 35 and losing only three. The losses, early in his career, were temporary setbacks and soon forgotten. From 1805–1812 he had beaten armies from the triumvirate of Austria, Russia and Prussia decisively. This impressive track record gave Napoleon a sense of invincibility. His military genius undoubtedly affected the balance of continental power: in battle he was seen as a 'force multiplier', winning against the odds. He could inspire troops to superhuman efforts and terrify opponents.

Napoleon is regarded as a great military leader, still with lessons for today. There is no evidence that he read the great Chinese military classic by Sun Tzu, but the practical insights into fighting battles offered by the Chinese strategist were frequently matched in Napoleon's approach to military conquest. Napoleon appreciated the value of having a competitive advantage (which need not be weight of numbers) and that success meant making fewer mistakes than the enemy. Napoleon's *levée en masse* can be seen as comparable with a natural organization, with advantages over more structured units. His armies had a clearly defined purpose in each battle; Napoleon was well-informed, well-prepared and strategically flexible. Like Sun Tzu, Napoleon focused on knowing the facts, gaining inside information, making detailed preparations and planning. His childhood experiences in Corsica prepared him for different terrain and challenging fighting conditions. Like Sun Tzu, Napoleon concentrated on seizing the day, operating quickly and proactively, favouring the attacking mode much more than being defensive. Sun Tzu advised leaders to expect the worst, and Napoleon had no illusions about the quality and quantity of what he was often up against. The Austrian armies in particular were well-paid, well-equipped, large and efficient. So Napoleon knew that his innovations in strategy, the advantage of surprise, his ability to move fast and keep on the march could be essential to success. He could not fight on the same terms as his opponents so, as practiced by Sun Tzu, he would be faster, better and would keep them guessing. He would burn bridges and avoid retreat; this strategy was finally used against him by the Russians, with the result that the retreat from Moscow was especially costly for the defeated French forces.

Napoleon certainly used meritocratic criteria in building his army, which may be contrasted with other ways of selecting people for promotion: nepotism, oligarchy, plutocracy, aristocracy, for example. Meritocracies often contrast elaborate modes of examination and certification, valuing formal qualifications as indicators of merit. These contribute to the perceived legitimacy of office-holders, though practical achievements are also valued.

Merit is most easily displayed in the context of a specialist skill or area of knowledge. Leadership that draws on this kind of expertise has a distinct advantage: it makes sense to ask the expert to take charge. At the very least, other specialists are more likely to respect and follow someone whose knowledge and skill they recognize. But of course, not every geek makes a good leader. Some of this is simply because the expertise learned in mastering a specialist set of skills and knowledge might have little to do with handling groups of people. Leadership inevitably places the leader in a position of facing outwards towards an environment which is not controllable, by contrast quite the opposite of detailed specialist work. And in any sizeable organization, internal politics becomes an overriding concern for anyone trying to develop and protect a project, a department or a whole business. At higher levels, political savvy becomes the most relevant expertise.

The idea of a meritocracy is probably the dominant assumption in modern organizations: ability to do the job is the best reason for promoting someone to be in charge. Measuring and assessing this ability is not always straightforward. Someone who knows a lot in theory might not be so good at putting it into practice; someone who proves to be very capable in practice might actually be drawing support from other team members, and be less effective when placed in authority above them.

While it is easy enough to assess competency in observable skills, the things that matter in leadership are often hard to measure: for example, although most people say that integrity and authenticity are very important qualities in leadership, they are not easily assessed by formal objective measures. This is why many leadership assessment processes turn to 360-degree feedback approaches, inviting close colleagues to comment from their experience of working with the person.

The ideal of a meritocracy was not new in Napoleon's time – it was the core idea of Confucian reforms in the fourth century. But it was rare: the eighteenth-century British navy was unusually meritocratic, recruiting people from all classes of society into the officer ranks based (substantially) on merit. The British army was different: officers were exclusively aristocratic, sharply separated from the soldierly mass. The French Revolution had done away with aristocrats, but there was already an admission that officers needed some training to boost the authority that was supposedly a natural corollary of noble birth. The military academy from which Napoleon graduated as an artillery officer was founded just as the *ancien régime* collapsed, and it instituted a curriculum with tests and examinations. Napoleon was particularly gifted at geometry, essential in calculating the arc of fire for artillery. At any other time in France, such qualifications would not have been enough to earn a place in the officer ranks without the foundation of aristocratic origins.

Meritocracy, then, is not an exclusively modern ideal, but it has become the dominant assumption – so much so that breaches are treated as moral failures. Discriminating between candidates on the basis of anything other than merit (class, race, gender, tribe, clan) is seen today as scandalously improper in most parts of the world. The ideal is even enshrined in the Universal Declaration of Human Rights: 'All people are born equal ...', and Equal Opportunities policies prevail in many workplaces.

This is all good, of course, but there are limitations to meritocracy as a description of what actually happens; and as a pathway to power, it is seldom enough. First, most work is accomplished in relation with others, by co-ordination of tasks and active co-operation amongst people. This entails trust, which depends on more than the qualifications, skills and knowledge of individuals. Trusting relations depend on a shared subjective sense of commonality: people tend to trust members of their in-group, which means people they see as like themselves. Conversely, they mistrust out-groups – those who are different.

Second, meritocracy threatens the privileged classes much as it did in revolutionary France. Equal opportunities practices aim to bring proven merit to the fore, but privilege is usually institutionalized in myriad ways into the way organizations work: who is included in the privileged communications, the timing of the working day, even the physical layout of facilities. The people in power need do nothing: the whole system makes sure only the 'right' people get in.

Third, meritocracy appeals to a certain kind of rationality, sometimes called 'instrumental rationality', on the assumption that people have clearly defined goals and standards, that they know what is required in order to achieve these, and that they can select the inputs to produce those ends. It is a set of assumptions well described as 'instrumental', in which ends or purposes, and the means to attain them, are thought to be closely coupled: if we do x, y will follow; and if we want y, we should do x. So if we want to win wars we need great generals, and to get these we should provide certain kinds of training. Therefore people who succeed in that training should be appointed as generals, and they will win wars.

But this is a set of assumptions with only a limited applicability. Cause and effect seldom work like this. Taking the example above, there are many reasons why wars are won or lost; the quality of generals is just one of them, and training is just one of the factors influencing how generals turn out in practice.

There are many advantages of expert leadership and using the power gained by merit. These include being noticed and increasing your expert power, and leveraging your perceived outstanding ability, especially when you know far more about what you are doing than most people around you.

But the disadvantages can include being typecast in this mould. Others might think this is the only thing you're good at, and that you might have difficulties in trying to see the world from other perspectives. They might assume that you have a level of naïve simplicity – the mistake of seeing Napoleon as a simple soldier. Expert leaders face the danger of seeing people who are less expert and meritorious than they are, as of limited utility, and discounting their potential contributions in other areas.

Question on leadership and power

To what extent must you prove your merit and ability, in order to get ahead?

- Choose a much sought-after and much-needed area of specialization in your career to start with – to get you started on the ladder to power.

- Don't hang around – get noticed early in your career, power can take a while to be accumulated.

- Be in a small minority with your value-added skill when it's needed the most – and be ready to seize opportunities.

- Having incompetent superiors can work in your favour – but don't show them up, help them to cover-up and let them think they are still powerful.

- Make the most of your contacts, however few and local – you can get lucky here.

- Get help to make a showy promotion of yourself and then broadcast the news.

- See your own potential and where you could go – don't wait for others to help you.

- Rise above your area of specialization as soon as you can – it's a tool for advancement, not an end in itself.

CHARISMA

Battles for Bridges – Lodi/Arcola, 1796: the appeal and dangers of charismatic leadership

I will lead you into the most fertile plains in the world. Rich provinces and great cities will be in your power. There you will find honour, glory and wealth.

Napoleon, letter to his soldiers, 1795

In vain did the generals, knowing the importance of time, rush to the front to force our columns across the little bridge ... we had to cross this bridge or make a detour of several leagues which would have nullified our whole operation. I went up myself and asked the soldiers if they were still the victors of Lodi: my presence had an effect that decided us to attempt the crossing once more.

Napoleon at Arcola, 1797

We suddenly saw him appear on the embankment, surrounded by his general staff and followed by his guides, he dismounted, drew his sword, took the flag and rushed into the middle of the bridge amid a rain of fire.

Napoleon at Arcola, Dwyer, 2007, p2

Napoleon's presence on the battlefield is worth 40,000 men.

Wellington, 1809, p412

The imperatives of charismatic leadership do not permit a benign abdication of such men in the face of an era of peace and pluralistic democracy.

McLynn, 1998, p664

Napoleon tried to enhance his own charisma with propaganda and image-creation, creating an idealized portrait of how he wanted to appear. In the early days of his career he had only had merit but no networks. He was a poor officer from the colonies without connections.

Dwyer, 2007, pp515–517

The Italian campaign was a brilliant opportunity for Napoleon to demonstrate his courage and bravery in the field, his campaigning genius and his exceptional good luck. At the Battle of Lodi and on the Bridge of Arcola he seemed to be inspired and protected beyond normal mortals, and thus began the process of creating his legend. His tremendous work ethic and attention to detail meant that he was always a progenitor of events, and when everything else is in flux a leader who takes initiative is immensely attractive – and can be seen as charismatic for this reason alone.

Early in his career Napoleon benefited from patronage to escape provincial obscurity, access an excellent education and obtain his first military appointments. He had demonstrated his abilities as an artillery officer, a planner and field commander. But as we shall see in this chapter, Napoleon was able to produce something extraordinary from these advantages and talents. There was no shortage of young men with initiative in revolutionary France, before any semblance of political stability was achieved in the country, but Napoleon was outstanding. He managed to avoid the many risks of political instability, and worked his way into a daring military venture that became the crucible for his transformation into a remarkable charismatic leader.

As a rising young General known for victories in the field of battle defending France and the Revolution, Napoleon was sent by the Convention, then leading France, to take command of the first Italian campaign in March 1796. He had just married Josephine. Life was exciting and full of promise. He had been liberated from imprisonment in the dark days of his affiliation with the Robespierres, when Paris was in turmoil. He had been restored to his position in the army, and in Paris he had worked hard to establish important contacts and build a name for

himself socially and politically. He had particularly made his mark when
he had been appointed by the Convention to help Paul Barras, one of the
Directors, to subdue a Royalist rising in Paris. It was therefore through
Barras that Napoleon was given command of the army destined for Italy,
and through Barras that Napoleon had met Josephine, a well-connected
socialite whose salon entertained the great and the good.

Through victories in the north of Italy (especially Lodi, Arcola and then
Rivoli) Napoleon was to establish his reputation as the first great general
of the Republican armies. This was at a time when incursions were being
made by the Austrians into France's borders. These wars were genuinely
defensive, reflecting the response of France's neighbours, and threatened
to undermine France whilst she was still politically weak and suffering constant changes in leadership, and could have even overturned the
gains of the Revolution. This was a crucial turning-point in the early,
unstable years of post-revolutionary France, when Royalists within
France were being supported by enemies without, as we have seen in the
case of Toulon.

Napoleon had been given command of France's secondary army in a pin-
cer offensive against Austria in 1796, and was then promoted, due to his
success in attacking the Austrians in Italy head-on. The Directory, succeeding the Convention, under accusations of corruption and in a state
of chaos, was anxious to defend France against invaders and put some
victories behind its name to build its reputation. Remarkably, even as a
very young officer, Napoleon was seen as one of France's most senior
military officers, to the extent that eventually he was to confidently
dictate the peace terms to the Austrians at Campo-Formio on the conclusion of these hostilities. Here we focus on two battles in particular, Lodi
and Arcola, as early examples of Napoleon's charisma in the field, which
also help explain his rising status and recognition.

What was the background to this campaign? The Austrian army under
General Alvinzy had enabled Austria to hold Mantua and dominate
much of Italy. Napoleon had already compelled the King of Sardinia to
conclude an armistice by threatening Turin, and had made a triumphal
entry into Milan after the Battle of Lodi in May 1796, followed soon
after by the Battle of Arcola in November.

By 1797, Jacques-Louis David's pictures of the dashing young Napoleon
crossing the Alps, deliberately resembling a latter-day Hannibal, had
fired the public imagination. These paintings illustrated a succession of
French victories: at Castiglione (August 1796), Bassano (September),
Arcola (November) and Rivoli (January 1797), and engravings were

eagerly snapped up on the streets of Paris. Of especially dramatic appeal had been Napoleon's triumphal entry into Milan after the Battle of Lodi on 10 May 1796.

What happened specifically at the Battle of Lodi which exemplified Napoleon's charismatic appeal? Following the April 1796 armistice with the Piedmontese, the Austrians were forced into retreat. There was one bridge across the River Adda, at the little town of Lodi, as Napoleon, marching there in May 1796, prepared to again give battle to the Austrians.

The bridge at Lodi was made from wooden piles, 200 yards long and 12 feet wide. Storming this bridge, heavily defended by the enemy, was a risky if not suicidal venture. The Austrian guns were firing steadily as Napoleon quickly considered the possibilities of success. Convinced he must go ahead, he raced across the bridge on his stunning white horse under heavy fire, calling for his soldiers to follow. There was no precedent for such a tactic, and Napoleon's almost inexplicable survival was seen as amazing by both sides. Combined with a diversionary flanking movement of his cavalry on the Austrian right, and simultaneously bringing his infantry into the town square, the enemy were overwhelmed.

Having overcome the heavy odds that he might fall in battle, Napoleon appeared as an almost messianic figure, working up the troops to fever pitch. Playing *la Marseillaise*, and leading his soldiers from the front whilst his white horse could be seen for miles, Napoleon's dramatic rush across the bridge brought an immediate response from the Austrians, who were then attacking the bridge from all angles. The French soldiers, under extremely heavy fire, were frequently forced to jump into the water to avoid the rain of musketry. Yet the French army made it across in sufficient numbers to turn the tide of the battle. So Lodi was a very dramatic victory, with Napoleon in the thick of the fighting, placing the guns and as well as leading the column across the bridge. As the French cavalry finally appeared on the Austrian right to back them up, the Austrian rear guard abandoned the bridge and retreated. Napoleon then entered Milan in triumph.

The Battle of Lodi remained in Napoleon's mind as a psychological landmark in his career and marks a new stage in his development as a charismatic leader. Against all the odds and the prospect of almost certain death, he incited soldiers to extremes of courage. At Lodi, for the first time, Napoleon became aware of the strength of his powers of leadership. Convinced of his special talents, ambitions and sense of mission, he realized he had the ability to gain support in extreme circumstances.

Later in the Italian War, the Battle of Arcola, in November 1796, involved a similar bridge-storming exercise. The experience reinforced Napoleon's conviction of his special talents in inspiring men to victory through his physical presence; even more, the soldiers could see it too. Arcola was one of the most dangerous battles for Napoleon, and came to a head after a forced march of 70 miles in two days. In this campaign he had experienced some defeats, had admitted to himself that he was losing heart, and realized that desperate measures were needed.

Watching the Austrians closely as they were moving down the River Adige south of Verona, Napoleon had been able to crush many of their units in a series of battles. Reaching Arcola, Napoleon put himself in more personal danger, and his ability to survive unscathed again added to his almost messianic image. Napoleon's horse was shot under him, this time plunging him into a swamp. Shoulder-deep in black mud and under heavy enemy fire, miraculously he was rescued and continued to fight.

In a daring flank march against the enemy rear across the river, Napoleon found he could not achieve the element of surprise for which he was planning – the enemy could already see him. A fierce Croat detachment defending the village and bridge of Arcola caused Napoleon an extra three days of heavy and costly fighting, across treacherous marsh and dykes. Napoleon had achieved a high level of motivation of his men but they couldn't keep going for ever. A Polish officer (an aide to Napoleon) described how he saw his much-admired General dramatically raise the French army standard on the bridge of Arcola, condemning the cowardice of the troops for not responding and taunting them to follow him. This dramatic moment became a romanticized theme for artists, but realistically this was a costly engagement and won by the narrowest of margins. But it turned out to be crucial for the campaign, as it paved the way for the Battle of Rivoli and the ultimate conquest of Mantua.

So the Directory, having replaced the Committee of Public Safety and the Convention and at this point in charge of the government and adminis-tration of France, were now receiving regular dispatches from the field of battle about the heroic General Bonaparte. Charisma can only be power-ful if well advertised, especially at a time of limited media development. However, the Directors were becoming increasingly worried about the independent streak Napoleon was exhibiting. Acting autonomously as demanded by the changing needs of battle, Napoleon officially denied being ambitious. But the Directory saw him as increasingly politically dan-gerous. Observers mentioned that he was 'feared, loved and respected in Italy' but was 'hard, impatient, abrupt, imperious' … and 'not respectful to Government commissioners' (Cronin, 1971: 148). Napoleon's response was that 'he could not possibly treat otherwise men who were universally scorned for their immorality and incapacity'.

Napoleon was intolerant of the profiteering and incompetence he was seeing around him. Saliceti, Napoleon's family friend from Corsica, was also involved in these wars, but he saw battles as opportunities for personal loot and much-needed to fund the impoverished Directory. Napoleon was to take a different line: he genuinely wanted the Italians to feel liberated, and to be part of the revolutionary gains, then being spread beyond the borders of France.

In mid-January 1797, at the Battle of Rivoli, Napoleon's first Italian campaign was to come to a brilliant conclusion. Again on the banks of the Rive Adige, this time 20 miles north of Verona and 10 miles east of Lake Garda, Napoleon (still only 27) directed the route of an entire Austrian army, led by a general with much more experience. By separating the infantry from the artillery and preventing different units from supporting each other, and especially stopping the artillery from providing cover for the highly exposed infantry in the field, Napoleon was able to force the Austrians into retreat. The French forces then captured Mantua, broke up the Austrian bases, replenished their own supplies and stopped the Austrians from further attacks on the French borders. This time there was no dispute that Napoleon was the man of the moment.

The Treaty of Campo Formio in October 1797 was significant in several ways: it was the first major 'land-grab' by post-revolutionary France; it replaced vassals of the Austrian empire with local bourgeois governments; and it gave Napoleon the experience of making peace on the back of military victory. He almost instantly represented a resurgent nation, the hero of *la Patrie*; and personified the transcendent ideas of liberty and equality that so excited the new bourgeoisie and terrified the colonial empires of Austria and Britain. Napoleon's army had fought with zeal and growing confidence that their cause was about something more than land and food. Their young General, leading them to victory and imposing peace, became the glorified recipient of their projected hopes that the horrors of the Revolution might actually presage a new and better world. By the end of this first Italian campaign, Napoleon had all the ingredients for charismatic leadership: a thrilling sense of his own exceptional competence, a conviction that he was an agent of historical destiny, and an army that wanted to believe it too.

The irony is evident only in hindsight: as a champion of the egalitarian rationalism that had swept away the *ancien régime*, he was to become one of the most totalitarian rulers in Europe. As a statesman, he never learned to negotiate a treaty without military domination, and so doomed much of Europe to war and destruction for another 20 years, and the final treaties that shaped the modern continent were made without him.

Reflections on leadership and power

- Napoleon was never a quiet leader, he was always at the front line.
- His role on the battlefield was seen by his enemies as an essential ingredient in his army's success.
- He was always visible, to inspire the soldiers.
- His visibility helped make sure the battles went according to plan.
- His presence also suggests a possible lack of trust and confidence in those around him, and reluctance to delegate.
- He was visible to avoid being disappointed by a reliance on initiative of others.
- Napoleon relied on his personal charisma to push people and keep them going when their motivation was flagging.

Napoleon's emerging prowess as a military leader and the increasing exposure of France and her enemies to his charisma was based on several important factors. First, he built up his military expertise and increased his chances of victory through intense planning and preparation, though he never let this limit his willingness to 'go for it'. As he pointed out, 'few people realize the strength of mind required to conduct, with a full realization of its consequences, one of these great battles on which depends the fate of an army, a nation, the possession of a throne. Consequently one rarely finds Generals who are keen to give battle' (Markham, 1963: 39–40).

Second, he realized what was at stake in the practical issues of conducting warfare and strategy; this could not be simply reduced to a formula or a system, and could not easily be quantified. Napoleon did not agree with many of the maxims of war extolled in the literature, considering them impossible to put into practice. The textbook approach to warfare might only work if the army was in an ideal condition. From the outset, he realized that the main problem in post-revolutionary France was the state of the army: 'One battalion has mutinied on the grounds that it had neither boots nor pay ... the army is in frightening penury ... misery has led to indiscipline' (Markham, 1963: 40–41). Napoleon immediately spent gold on bread, meat, brandy and especially on boots.

The basic matters of food and clothing had to be addressed first before any fancy battle strategies could be employed, especially because many of Napoleon's enemies 'wanted for nothing', particularly the wealthy Austrians. Napoleon's ability to identify key practical problems and deal with them was an important precursor to victory in the field – and was an essential foundation and accompaniment to charisma.

Third, Napoleon's published proclamations and speeches to his soldiers in the field aimed to be inspirational and, combined with his charismatic personality, frequently hit the spot: 'I will lead you into the most fertile plains in the world. Rich provinces and great cities will be in your power. There you will find honour, glory and wealth' (Markham, 1963: 41). This kind of inspirational address was more powerful than strategy and general maxims of war. It was especially powerful for soldiers who suddenly and unexpectedly found they had food in their stomachs, uniforms on their backs and gold in their pockets. This was amazing!

Another aspect of Napoleon's charisma, and in this way he was noticeably different from many other officers, was his personal energy and high level of output and activity. Observers at the time thought this came from his broad chest and big lungs, which meant that he did everything quickly. Perhaps this was developed through climbing the hills of Corsica from a young age. We have already seen that he could get by on very little sleep; he was renowned for his ability to sleep for half an hour wrapped up in his cloak and then keep going for up to 24 hours.

Fourth, Napoleon knew topography. As part of his Corsican heritage, he had an instinctive sensitivity (not just lung capacity) for mountainous terrain, such as the shape and line of hills. As a gunner by training, he could concentrate on one point on the landscape, take it by storm, and then move on to another. Sometimes he realized that it would be better to follow the coast rather than the mountains, and made quick decisions based on practical criteria. With rapid speed, and being well-synchronized, Napoleon's troops began to win – nearly every time. In 96 hours in the Italian Wars his unit was able to win four battles up and down steep foothills: so they were certainly in a position to be able to dictate peace terms, with a shocked and scattered enemy unused to losing and reeling from the blows inflicted by the French.

The Italian campaign of 1796–97 gave Napoleon the opportunity to graphically show courage and bravery in the field: he was lucky to survive and, along with thousands of others, came to believe that this marked him out as someone with a special destiny, a 'charism' or gift from heaven. It all played into the hands of his mounting ambition.

At the Battle of Lodi, he showed strong practical leadership talent, and at the Bridge of Arcola created a legend.

By early 1797, he had become a well-known figure in French and European military issues, and therefore in politics. He was influencing the formation of international alliances through his own strategic accomplishments in the field. An Austrian envoy admitted that 'only Bonaparte can make peace, and he can do it on any terms he wants'. Augereau, a fellow French general, reflected that 'I can't understand it – that little bugger makes me afraid' (Cronin, 1971: 136).

Growing in Napoleon's mind was the idea that victory in battle was giving him influence in the Directory – and this exciting feeling was compensating for the disappointing lack of love and attention from Josephine. As he faced inner turmoil and stress and was restless and anxious over the perceived failure of his marriage (she frequently failed to answer his letters for weeks and was known to be in the company of other dashing, good-looking officers), the Directory was concerned about his increasing power. They were considering dividing his command and appointing another general to keep him in check. Napoleon responded by threatening to resign and they drew back, especially as the Directory increasingly wanted Italy for plunder. Worried about where the money was going and how much he could keep, Napoleon started paying his troops half their pay in silver.

So, at a time of the desperate financial weakness of the Directory, Napoleon had charisma and silver. This was a powerful combination. He and the other generals in the field were flexing their muscles. This was a very different story from the earlier period of rule of the Committee of Public Safety, before the Directory, when outspoken and difficult generals could be easily dismissed by politicians. By contrast, the Directory was becoming dependent for its existence on the success of its military and the pro-Republican spirit of its armies. In the Italian Wars, it soon became clear that, liberated from Austria, Italian discontent and rebellion meant that these wars were not about military domination but about politics – the next frontier for Napoleon.

Many of Napoleon's enemies were not at all keen to give battle, especially as his reputation grew. Avoiding pitched battles with Napoleon became a sensible policy. But then they became the way for France – through Napoleon – to expand her territories beyond her borders. Defending French territory against incursions soon gave way to proactively acquiring new lands and expanding France's borders.

Although awkward socially, especially evident during his early days when courting Josephine, Napoleon was an attractive character to fellow officers and soldiers. Never a quiet leader, he was always at the front – he felt he had to be (and it was anyway not possible to be too far back and still be able to communicate with the troops). The importance of his presence was confirmed by his enemies, who resigned themselves to defeat when he personally led armies, not just because he was brilliant but also because he was charismatic.

Napoleon felt he must always be visible to his soldiers, and not only to inspire them. It also suggests that he lacked confidence in his subordinate officers, which he felt was often justified, as he was frequently disappointed when he relied on others. They didn't turn up, they waited too long to take action, and they were distracted by opportunities for pillaging. His followers performed best if he was there at the front with them, sharing their triumphs as well as their hardships. He relied heavily on his own personal charisma to push people when their motivation was flagging and defeat seemed likely, and this always had to be face to face.

The advantages of leading from the front include control, heightened power, a sense of knowing what's going on, being able to influence events; but the disadvantages can include reluctance to delegate, and a failure to develop talents and a sense of responsibility in others. If the charismatic leader is always there, and the leader's charismatic power is eclipsing everyone else's, those around the leader abandon their own initiative and leave everything to the leader. Napoleon soon stopped wondering why he ended up doing everything himself.

Napoleon's charisma was later to turn to narcissism. Influenced by the grandeur of the Italian campaign and his time in Egypt and by the uncritical attitude of most of his followers, his narcissism grew with every battle. He took personal credit for every win, and uncritically accepted the accolades heaped on him every day. Thus, he failed to face changing realities, rejected the need to change his plans and was unwilling to see the obvious. Continued success in the use of power can lead to hubris – when 'pride comes before a fall'. Observers at the time and later, saw him as a slave to his narcissism, provoked by the adulation of his followers, and resulting in a callous indifference to human life in the pursuit of his ambition to constantly expand his power.

Charisma, in whatever form it takes, can possess a person, as it is projected on them by others. With no television or megaphones, a leader could only speak to a small number of people at a time. But belief in the charisma of a leader could replace actual contact with him. Charisma therefore can be seen as a form of power: people feel themselves to be moved, inspired and captivated by the extraordinary personality of a charismatic person.

In the modern era, conservation movements speak of charismatic species of animals: lions, elephants, dolphins and whales are described as unusually present and compelling. They seem to evoke something beyond the human scale, something more glorious, wonderful and beautiful. The word 'charisma' is literally derived from the Greek word for 'a gift of the gods'.

A charismatic person is believed to carry this divine gift, to evoke the superhuman, and in an emotional sense reminds people of purposes beyond short-term instrumentalism. It seems to refer to ideals beyond possible human realization. Being in the presence of a charismatic leader, it is possible to feel that ordinary acts of war or business are converted, even transmuted, into something significant, more noble, than they first appeared.

Many writers on charisma assume it to be a quality of exceptional human beings, but it is more properly understood as a phenomenon available to humanity and only sometimes realized. Charisma is seen not in the context that a person has it, but has evoked it. Charisma is enabled in some circumstances; it is an experience between people. It is not that one person just has it; it is the result of a catalyst.

Napoleon was often the centre of a charismatic event, like addressing his soldiers at the foot of the Pyramids in Egypt. The phenomenon of charisma at this moment cannot be explained entirely by his personal presence amongst others. Commanding armies of hundreds of thousands of soldiers, without videos or photography or artificial amplification, there must have been many who followed him and never saw him and never heard his voice, but they knew his charismatic presence by reputation. He figured in their imagination through the stories told about him, passed between soldiers orally during long marches.

This charismatic presence followed him beyond France. On his abdication, English people flocked to catch a glimpse of him as a prisoner on board HMS *Bellerophon* in spite of orchestrated attempts by the authorities to turn him into an object of ridicule, based on his small stature, supposed impotence and experience of female rejection. By contrast, the French iconography focuses on the paintings produced to create the heroic image, especially that by David, of Napoleon crossing the Alps in a deliberate parody of Hannibal. Another insightful painting during the period of image creation is that of Gros' 'Visiting the Plague-Stricken in Jaffa', which literally features Napoleon healing the sick by touching. The industry in France for messianic Napoleon images did not come to an end with his death; a painting by Jazet of Napoleon leaving his tomb in the Invalides of 1840 was produced at a time of chaos and uncertainty when the return of Napoleon was a longed-for dream.

The visual iconography of Napoleon was accompanied by powerful rhetoric. He wrote evocative prose and made marvellous speeches, which were written down and reprinted, speeches which poetically captured dramatic moments. At his first abdication, at the defeat of 1814, Napoleon took leave of his beloved National Guard in the theatrical setting of the courtyard of Fontainebleu. This moment still evokes the pathos of the great man, brought low by virtue of his own greatness, in the classical tradition of tragedy.

A tragic ending may also have charismatic influence, as it links the protagonists to profoundly super-human themes. In classical and Shakespearean tragedy, for example, the good people are brought low along with the bad. Everyone loses everything. Yet the impression is not one of outrageous unfairness; rather that when there is evil in the system, it has a toxic effect. The system itself, the order of the world, must therefore be fundamentally opposed to evil, and this explains why tragic theatre is cathartic and life-affirming rather than depressingly nihilistic. At the end of Shakespeare's *King Lear* audiences long for Cordelia to live and Lear to be revived, but know this to be a romantic wish. The longed-for happy ending may help to explain a curious event: when in 1815 Napoleon landed back in France from exile in Elba, the forces sent to arrest him turned to his support, as did thousands who rallied to his cause on the way to Paris, abandoning the recent chance of peace. Most surely he knew this was an impossible resurrection of a hopelessly romantic dream, yet it was irresistible. The charisma to which they responded is largely, we suggest, a romantic enthusiasm, centred on an extraordinary person who seems to embody the possibility of transcending the ordinary world of fairness and equality, of living (and dying) in ways that hint at unconditioned greatness.

Napoleon's charisma had wide appeal down the centuries. The German philosopher Nietzsche saw him as embodying the qualities of an older, nobler time. Despising modernity, equality and nationalism, Nietzsche admired Napoleon's grandiose aspirations to create a pan-European culture and political arena. Nietzsche saw Napoleon as a 'higher man' – a political actor in an egalitarian era with a populist ethos who, though finally corrupted, stood for something greater than the common man. Napoleon was superhuman (*ubermensch*) but was also inhuman (*unmensch*): superhuman for whom he was, not what he did. His power of character made him one of the 'more profound and comprehensive men of this century' (Glenn, 2001: 133). To Nietzsche, Napoleon was the ultimate symbol of power: personifying the feeling of power, the will to power, and power in a man. He created for himself a coherent, total self, a powerful soul who refused to respect others, and was unwilling to be influenced by anyone, except perhaps some of his heroes from history – other charismatic leaders like Caesar, Hannibal and Charlemagne.

Questions on leadership and power

Must you lead from the front and be charismatic or can you practice quiet leadership, behind the scenes?

- Are you charismatic? This can be a useful trait but it's not everything.

- Decide if you want to be visible or behind the scenes – there are advantages in both.

- Know your core competency and added value – it may not involve being seen around all the time.

- How do you inspire people who work with you? You need to find your own way.

- How do you make sure your plans are put into action?

- What is your attitude to trust and delegation? Are you aware of the advantages and disadvantages of each?

- What do you do when backs are against the wall and the situation is looking grim? What is your fall-back mode in a difficult situation?

COUP D'ETAT

Brumaire and end of the Directory, 1799: the precariousness of hanging on to seized power

There is your man, he will make your coup d'état.

Director Sieyès, of Napoleon at Brumaire, 1799

Napoleon had ruthless ambition, enough to seize power when others just stood around; he had 'le courage de l'improviste', *spontaneous courage.*

Dwyer, 2007, p21

Neither red cap nor red heel, I represent the nation.

Napoleon, 11 November 1799

Napoleon is the mightiest breath of life that ever quickened human clay.

Chateaubriand, 1800

Napoleon's plan for a legal change of government hadn't worked but in the end it turned to Napoleon's advantage. He had used force reluctantly and not much of it – and now he was a consul, and now had the opportunity to help write the new constitution of France.

Cronin, 1971, pp212–213

In the coup d'état or putsch of Brumaire in November 1799 (after the French revolutionary calendar name for that month), Napoleon opportunistically seized power to become a consul and eventually to be First Consul, and then Consul for Life. A big build-up of the pro-Bonaparte lobby had been taking place in recent months, with Napoleon positioning himself in the public eye for political power. His dramatic victories in Italy, described in the official reports he sent to Paris, came after exotic tales reported from Egypt, such as 'Bonaparte is advancing on India, and now on Constantinople'. Journalists had been in the pay of the Bonaparte family for several years, and Napoleon was to exert tight control over the media throughout his career. When he seized power he was seen by many as the personification of an emerging and renewed France. From this point he concentrated more and more power in his direct control. The achievement of this coup d'état, this putsch, is the subject of this chapter.

Napoleon became embroiled in the Brumaire coup that brought down the existing government, the Directory, and at the same time brought him into a much more powerful leadership role than ever before. Named after the 'foggy month' in the new calendar names adopted by the French Revolutionaries in 1789, this coup was one of the most important turning points in his career. Between 1799 and 1804 he became the autocrat of France and all the dependent territories that his conquests had secured for her – a power he held on to for another decade.

The parliamentary chambers had been summoned by the Directory to Saint-Cloud, just outside Paris, to avoid the unpredictable and potentially violent Paris mob. Napoleon, as a military leader, was appointed to provide security for the move and ensure the peaceful operation of the chambers of deputies there. This he saw as a chance to use his official position to try to break the political deadlock by staging a putsch. Through engaging the intervention of his brother Lucien – voted onto the Council of Five Hundred through the growing influence of the Bonaparte name – Napoleon realized that he could induce the Council of Elders and the Council of Five Hundred to eventually disperse from their chambers. He could then undermine the power of the Directory to such a degree that they would step aside and allow the three provisional consuls to be appointed (Napoleon, Sieyès and Ducos) as part of a new constitution. Then it would be only a matter of time before Napoleon would out-manoeuvre the other two and concentrate power into his own hands. Although Napoleon thought through the coup d'état as he would think through and plan a military campaign, it did not quite work out in the way he intended. It could be said that coups and putschs are usually no more straightforward than battles.

The process of Napoleon seizing power had started in 1799 when, leaving his armies trapped behind him in Egypt, he had returned to France to protect his interests in the midst of political chaos. In fact, the Directors had decided to summon Napoleon home with his army, but he had left Egypt before receiving their summons, and had been unable to evacuate the army because his fleet had been destroyed by Nelson's squadron in the previous year, in 1798. This was not the only time he was to leave an army behind him, but the popular enthusiasm and acclaim he received all the way to Paris seemed to absolve him of any crime. The people still remembered Campo Formio and the satisfaction of dealing with the much-disliked Austrians from a position of strength.

Napoleon was influential with soldiers and the masses, but his appeal was not necessarily well received by political sophisticates such as the Directory. Some members thought he should be arrested for deserting the army; but the Directory itself was already discredited on account of its domestic inefficiencies, and its inability to prevent diplomatic reversals such as Tsar Paul of Russia's new anti-French alliance with Austria. The Directory, facing debt and inflation and enemies at its borders, had wanted to keep the new possessions in Italy, mostly to financially exploit them. Napoleon's General Massena had been put in charge in Rome but things were going wrong; King Ferdinand had been forced to leave Naples for Sicily and great chaos had ensued; an Austro-Russian army was back in Milan despite Napoleon's gains; but Napoleon himself wasn't criticized – it was the Directory that was seen as weak and corrupt.

Director Joseph Sieyès, to become one of the three consuls of the Consulate following the demise of the Directory, was one of few leaders still respected in France and regarded as espousing the values of the Revolution. Seen as moderate and reasonable, he was looking for a general ('a sword') to influence his fellow Directors to create a new constitution. He had already identified Napoleon; many other generals had fled overseas, had been guillotined in the Terror or were otherwise discredited, so there was not a lot of choice. There was pressure by many in the councils to abandon the Directory and revive the Committee of Public Safety, but the Council of Elders and the Council of the Five Hundred had carried on. Lucien, Napoleon's brother, had become president of the latter based largely on his connection with Napoleon, and organized the Bonapartist party. Other supporters of Napoleon's bid to enter politics included ex-Bishop, ex-Minister Talleyrand (out of office and looking for a change in government to try his luck) and Roederer, an influential journalist.

Napoleon realized he had to work with Sieyès, but he did not want to join any factions and did not want to be used as a tool by others. One of his strengths was that he was able to resist being typecast, and he always tried to keep his options open. He was willing to chart his own path whilst others frequently sided with one group or another. Partly as a result of his struggle for acceptance in France as a foreigner, he had no natural allies beyond his family and his military comrades. So, at first, he accepted the appointment of at least three consuls to dilute the power of the others. But Sieyès, who hoped to control his military muscle, was beginning to question who would be the horse and who would be the rider?

Working together with Sieyès and Ducos, Napoleon relied on his personal charisma, the political impasse and his own active propaganda to win popular support. Sieyès was a moderate and widely acceptable member of the Directory, Ducos an active supporter. Together they chose a day for their proposed coup. The timing was also influenced by the appointment of Napoleon by the deputies to provide the military guard at Saint-Cloud. The would-be consuls decided that Napoleon would lead the coup and Sieyès and Ducos would be there when needed, with the planned outcome being a new constitution.

Meanwhile, through his media campaign over the previous few weeks, Napoleon had accused the Directors of being self-seeking, inactive and unconstitutional; provoking popular opinion through a poster campaign by Roederer pasted all over Paris. Napoleon was lucky that he arrived when Paris felt a palpable desire for someone to take control, with the different constitutional bodies in a state of flux. His preparations for the coup (unlike his preparations for a battle) were hasty, vague and unco-ordinated – though Josephine helped him to host back-to-back meetings with plotting parties from all factions, and called on her old contacts amongst many of the political elite. The principals, including Sieyès and Napoleon, had their own secret agendas, which they did not share: everyone was double-guessing what others would do. Seizing political power in France for Napoleon would mean working through politicians; this was not his forte. As a Corsican, his power of patronage in France was still limited; he was from a small, poor colony; and his ability lay in the clear hierarchies of military command.

With the move of the Councils to Saint-Cloud, it was agreed by the Directory that they should meet and carry on their business there and Napoleon, appointed to a security role, was to ensure their safety. Some feared the anger of the Paris mob; others were more worried – rightly, as it turned out – about being entirely in the hands of a military escort commanded by the ambitious General. Typically, Napoleon wanted more power than he had been given.

Without discussing it with anyone, Napoleon suddenly appeared in his general's uniform at the first session of the Council of Elders at Saint-Cloud, surrounded by his officers and soldiers. As he would do in battle, Napoleon started haranguing his audience; but this time the crowds were the Elders of the government, not soldiers. In a long and tedious speech in which he frequently lost the point, Napoleon complained about the incompetence of the Directory and kept pointing out his military achievements: 'I left you with conquests and no enemy now invades our frontiers' (Markham, 1963: 75).

Napoleon's intention was to steal the initiative from Sieyès and get in front of the Councils before him, but the Elders were not impressed with this excitable and garrulous young soldier surrounded by his fellows invading their chamber. What was he doing here? He was supposed to be only in charge of their personal security. The Elders saw their current task as voting for new Directors, not to change the constitution, therefore they were hostile when Napoleon strode into their hall and launched into his speech demanding more radical change than they were prepared to consider. Inexperienced with politicians, Napoleon was simply not able to hold his audience. Observers reflected that the Elders were waiting for a statesman, but instead found a soldier on the defensive, and then got fed up with him and pushed him out of their chamber.

The Saint-Cloud meetings continued, in a stormy mood and delayed by interruptions and arrivals and departures of members. Napoleon, now out of the Elders' session, was becoming impatient. Used to the speed and decisiveness of the battlefield and the job of commanding soldiers, now he was in the wrong place. He wanted to appear before the Council of the Five Hundred to bring the matter to a head, but again he chose the wrong approach. Entering their chamber on his own, he hoped to win them over with his oratory, despite his lack of success with the Elders.

When Napoleon strode into the meeting of the Council of the Five Hundred, the deputies reacted angrily, surrounding him and, accusing him of autocratic ambitions, made to attack him. He was rescued by his military guard, but ejected from the Chamber. Napoleon's brother Lucien, Chair of the Council, was on hand and made the tactically clever move of accusing the deputies surrounding Napoleon (noting that some of them were armed with daggers) as being in the pay of England to attack France's most famous general. It sounded credible, as it was known that France's enemies employed many spies in Paris and nearby.

Napoleon was then hustled out of the chamber, and the Five Hundred carried on discussing their opposition to him, accusing him of acting like a king. To try to diffuse the situation and buy time, Lucien took off his Council insignia in protest, thereby delaying the vote to officially outlaw his brother, which would have destroyed Napoleon's chances of seizing power. Lucien could see that the moment was ebbing away and sent a message to his older brother that he had only 10 minutes to act. Napoleon himself then reappeared, bloody and dishevelled, and quickly the rumour spread that there had been an assassination attempt. The guards, who were not under the command of Napoleon, then entered the chamber. Initially hesitating at the dilemma of which authority they should obey, they followed the General and thrust their fixed bayonets towards the Five Hundred. Most of the deputies fled. The Elders, still in session, recognized the emergency and agreed to the appointment of three consuls, including Napoleon.

Lucien was able to gain the ratification of a new constitution by the few remaining members of the Council of Five Hundred, and by late night on the 9 November (called the 'Brumaire coup') it was all over. The Directory was declared at an end, and so were the Councils. The appointment of the three consuls had been made without bloodshed.

Napoleon's original plan for influencing a legal change of government in his favour had not worked out as he had foreseen, but in the end the impromptu nature of the proceedings and his crashing into the council sessions had turned to his advantage. The perception was that he had used force reluctantly and not much of it; now he was a consul he could officially help write the new constitution. From then on he rapidly assumed more power, making the most of his access to the popular press. In comparison, the other consuls remained in the background, either cripplingly indecisive or simply recognizing their subordinate power.

Napoleon then issued a manifesto to be published in Paris. Carefully ignoring Lucien's role and not acknowledging his brother's contribution, Napoleon pointed out that this was not a military coup d'état, as he had not used the troops of the Paris garrison. But he had provoked violent hostility from the politicians; he had made ineffective and ill-judged appearances in the Council sessions; and he had clearly shown his dislike and distrust of political assemblies. As a result, his position was still precarious. Yet his military reputation bolstered his popular support, especially because public opinion had turned sharply against the Directory. So he had a strong basis for power from which he could accumulate more, but by different means.

Observers at the time, such as the intellectual socialite Madame de Staël, saw the coup of Brumaire as the beginning of the dictatorship of Napoleon.

From this point he was determined to do everything himself, he refused to admit discussion and opposition, and adopted a cavalier attitude to the law of the land. Madame de Staël, initially enthusiastic about the hero of Lodi and Arcola, the explorer of Egypt, went from disappointment to hostility. She had seen Napoleon as a scholar and romantic, but now his megalomaniac ambition was taking over. She was not alone in seeing 1799 as marking the end of revolutionary ideals of civilian government.

By contrast, others saw it as the start of a period of greatness for France, characterized as *la Gloire* and *l'Honneur*. In this view the coup of Brumaire was an essential and effective way to deal with the chaos in government. The Directory had shown itself to be irresolute and incompetent; many of the ideals of the Revolution had already been lost, and all the armies of Europe were ranged against the country's borders. Napoleon was seen as the man who shunned both Royalists and Jacobins (he didn't take sides) and the broad mass of public opinion supported his efforts. Most of the population was looking for stability after a decade of upheaval, and Napoleon stood for order and unity and peace based on strength. Ironically, many saw the Brumaire as saving the Revolution – and not counter-revolutionary – but in the long term it meant that France now faced almost continuous war as Napoleon needed an atmosphere of emergency in which to bolster his position.

Napoleon approached the constitution as malleable to his will, and open to a continuous series of reforms. His regime was to be based on militarization, on compromised liberty, on centralized control and on demagogy. Any critic was conveniently accused of being in the pay of England: in other words, there could be no loyal opposition. It was increasingly perceived that France had enjoyed more liberties under the *ancien régime* and the Bourbons than after the Brumaire.

Reflections on leadership and power

Napoleon became obsessively ambitious in the build-up to and after the Brumaire coup d'état:

- He had gained a taste for ruling a whole country – albeit one subjected to his military occupation. There was very little indication that he had any experience or enthusiasm for a plural society in which innovation can thrive.

(Continued)

(Continued)

- He was prepared to risk everything in a critical moment – but he also worked tirelessly to create that moment, ensuring that he was there with the army behind him.

- He drew his wife and family into his political manoeuvrings; although obsessed with love, he never compromised his own ambition for the sake of his family or anyone else.

- Despite reams of passionate love-letters to Josephine, expressing desire and devotion, he never achieved the stable family life he had sometimes imagined.

- Josephine's affairs had hurt him, and he retaliated with affairs of his own, but he didn't seek another marriage until politically expedient. He had no desire for a partnership of equals, and sex became more and more another form of domination.

- Overall, he became more callous, heartless and work-obsessed, and this was channelled into growing ambition.

Napoleon knew power could be possessed but not hoarded: it had to be constantly exercised. The *ancien régime* monarchs sat on secure thrones, their power legitimized by church and custom. But for a campaigning General, power had to be actual, not just potential, and measured in numbers of people entering into its composition: soldiers, citizens and whole populations of countries. Power is an effect as much as a cause, and refers always to itself: power begets more power.

Arguably, there were four elements influencing Napoleon's motivations for seizing power and staging a putsch at this point. First, as a migrant and having abandoned his native Corsica and thrown in his lot with France, Napoleon was disgusted at the sorry state of his new country. Second, barred from entering politics because of his youth, aware of his reputation as a man of action, he felt conscious of a popular authorization for independent initiative. Third, his Egyptian adventures gave him a taste for rule at a national level. And fourth, his disappointment with Josephine turned him from any dreams he might have had about domestic calm.

First, Napoleon was appalled at the chaos of France on his return from overseas battles. It was intolerable, and he wanted to do something about it. By early 1799, the economy was in trouble. Merchants and investors had fled the country (only to return in the relative peace and security of the consulate period). Aristocrats going into exile left many of their domestic staff and retainers penniless and without the means of support. Trade had collapsed. Lawlessness and banditry was on the increase: even under guard, Napoleon's baggage had been stolen on his way through France to Paris on his return from Egypt. Many people looked back to the monarchy with nostalgia. The Directory, the latest in a long line of attempts at democratic and constitutional rule in France, was regarded with distrust. Many politicians and observers struggled against the continuing chaos. Napoleon was frustrated and provoked to do something about it.

Second, Napoleon was becoming politically active, and had sought appointment as a member of the Directory. His opponents – those who feared that General Bonaparte was out of control – had used the 40+ age rule to keep him out. Yet he received a hero's welcome when he returned from the Orient (as Egypt and the surrounding region was then known) and travelled across France, reflecting his growing charisma as a success- ful general, campaign leader, treaty maker and colonial governor. He was beginning to personify the uniquely French concept of *la Gloire*. He then became convinced that he could marshal public opinion behind him; yet he was not in a position of sufficient political authority to stem the chaos and start making the big constitutional changes he wanted to see, and to promote the ideals of the Revolution he had espoused.

Third, Napoleon wanted to rule. He had gained confidence from his experience in Egypt, the scientific and cultural discoveries and coloniz- ing reforms he could impose. Though the overall outcome was doubtful militarily, it had given him the taste for autocratic rule on a national scale; in fact he had imagined himself another Alexander the Great, extending his rule across Asia Minor to India. He was beginning to see himself as a statesman. He cannot be said to have ruled Egypt as a king with deep commitment to all aspects of life in a country, or for any sustained period of time, but he enjoyed the power, and developed a taste for it.

Finally, it might be that Napoleon's private life had some bearing on his public ambitions. He was disillusioned with Josephine after their first five years of marriage, and with his absence from home on one campaign after another it meant that the excitement and feeling in his life was now coming from his role as a leader in politics and on the battlefield. There were still no children of his own, though he was a generous patron to his stepson and stepdaughter. Although Napoleon and Josephine had decided to put the past behind them and settle down to a new life, it was not the same as before. The romantic young Napoleon writing love stories such as *Clisson et Eugénie* was gone forever.

So Napoleon was on the lookout for an opportunity, and had the means and ambition to take it. The move to become First Consul and out-manoeuvre his opponents became almost inevitable. He was never good at what we now call work–life balance; in his personal life he was either fanatically obsessed with the idea of romantic love or threw himself into his work to cover his disappointment and disillusionment with his experience of love. His suspicions about Josephine's infidelity and her inability to give him the love and support he needed changed his atti-tude towards his personal relationships, and he became more callous and heartless, though he had always been work-obsessed. It could be argued that his failure to establish a mutually rewarding marriage and his continuing entanglement with his maternal family is associated with an intolerance of shared power. It is a common scenario to throw oneself into work to compensate for shortcomings in one's private life, and with Napoleon's energy levels and ambition there was then no stopping him. A more contented person may have been less ambitious; Napoleon may have enjoyed excitement, but contentment was a rare achievement.

As he accumulated power and wealth, Napoleon made no attempt to relax and avoid what today we would call the excesses of workaholism. Achieving work–life balance doesn't win any medals, and extremes of achievement are often associated with concentrated passion and obsession.

The concept of a coup d'état or putsch has a paradoxical relationship with the idea of stable government. It is an inherently non-constitutional and therefore illegitimate action, but is often justified as a way to estab-lish stability. It is always a grab for power in the interests of one party against others; it is anti-pluralistic by nature. After this coup, Napoleon avidly bolstered his defences against anyone else trying to do the same. For the next 15 years he had no need of such a risky grab for power, though when the time came to do it again, in 1815, he was still up for it.

A coup may be a violent and decisive move to seize power, or it can be slow and gradual and hardly noticed at the time, in the way that some dictators (and many administrations) in the past have gradually accumu-lated power almost without anyone noticing. Some coups remove those in power but maintain fundamental structures of the state and institu-tions; others remove all traditional instruments of power and replace them with new ones.

A coup d'état or putsch can be seen as like a mutiny on a grand scale: intolerably unsettling if accompanied by the radical reform of institutions and procedures, but probably accepted if accompanied by peace and stability. Many countries – then and now – have not arrived at settled, peaceful procedures for changing governments. The norms of democratic elections, of one-party succession or of dynastic inheritance are not universally accepted. Countries without these are characterized by successive power-grabs which can change the characters in charge, but the institutions and elites usually remain the same.

The fundamental problem is one of succession: Napoleon's legitimacy was always dependent on his current and immediate successes; and because revolutionary France was always under attack, he was mostly running a militarized state, dependent on winning war after war. With no established process of succession, a counter-coup would always be likely. Neither French public opinions nor Napoleon could countenance a return to the disputatious governments of Directory and its predecessors, hence the growing obsession with identifying an heir to Napoleon.

A significant problem with coups d'état is the impact on continuity in an organization or state. The ability or readiness to honour commitments from one group of leaders to the next can be destroyed by a coup. Debts run up by one administration can be ignored and cancelled by the next, crucially undermining trade and other multi-lateral international relations.

The circumstances of the Brumaire coup of 1799 were apparently exceptional, but now all too familiar: the government in turmoil, the country facing the continued uncertain legitimacy of its rulers, and internecine fighting and near civil war. Where the political establishment becomes absorbed in its own struggles, the military often steps in. Although Napoleon manoeuvred for a takeover, it was not so much a carefully planned operation as a messy, opportunistic series of decisions, none with clearly foreseeable outcomes, and the result could have gone in a completely different direction. It was touch-and-go, risky and spontaneous – and Napoleon's quite remarkable luck played a part in the outcome.

Questions on leadership and power

How do you manage excesses of passion and obsession? How can you deal with growing ambition? Is achieving work–life balance a need for you? If you suffer personal disappointments, do you tend to become workaholic, and look for more opportunities for power to offset this?

(Continued)

(Continued)

- When did you first notice in yourself an increasing tendency towards ambition? What motivated this? Was it suggested by a single incident?

- Have you ever led a takeover, a coup, a putsch – in the workplace or any other context? Do you admire people who do, or do you see it as horrifying?

- Have you set out to achieve work–life balance? What is the ultimate lifestyle you seek? Are you getting there?

- Do you use work to cover your disappointments with other aspects of your life?

- Do you receive the love and support you need? Or have you become cynical?

- Are you ambitious, enough to take risks in seizing more power, or are you fairly laid back?

MANIPULATION

The Concordat with the Pope, 1801: winning across Europe by playing off allies and enemies against each other

One particular Napoleonic characteristic is the playing off of one potential enemy against another.

An Austrian observer at the
Treaty of Campo-Formio, 1797

Napoleon always argued that he was still supporting the aims of the revolution, and defending France – 'in war, moral considerations account for three-quarters; the balance of actual forces only the other quarter'.

Napoleon, 27 August 1808

Callous towards others and the lives of others, Napoleon never hesitated to sacrifice the lives of others to promote his own ambition.

Dwyer, 2007 p516

There must be a religion for the people.

Napoleon, 1801

A new game is beginning, and Napoleon must win it. 'I revere the Pope, who is a man of great kindness ... and I wish to come to an agreement with him, but I cannot accept the changes you have been considering in Rome. You will be given another version of the agreement. It is absolutely imperative that you sign it within five days ...

or everything will be broken off and I will adopt a national religion.
Nothing will be easier for me to do than this'.

Napoleon to Cardinal Consalvi, July 1801

Fifty émigré bishops in English pay are the present leaders of the
French clergy. Their influence must be destroyed, and for this I must
have the authority of the Pope.

Napoleon, 1801

We must respect the Pope – and treat him as if he had 200,000 men.

Napoleon, 1801

The use of a form of power based on connivance and manipulation
became a feature of the Consulate regime after the Brumaire coup, with
the jockeying for position among the three consuls. This was resolved
only as Napoleon came to enjoy total power – which he gained to a
large degree with his election as Consul for Life in 1802, and Emperor
in 1804. The relationship between the French administration and the
Catholic Church (the subject of this chapter) was an area of particular
contention, featuring a series of contradictions and compromises settled
in a Concordat. A generic word for a treaty between the Papacy and a
temporal power, in this case the Concordat was an agreement between
Pope Pius VII and Napoleon of July 1801.

In the early days of the Revolution, Church lands were nationalized and churches themselves converted to 'Temples of Reason'. How
could the government reduce the power of the Papacy but not appear
in opposition to the most popular religion? As a leader becoming
more and more autocratic, Napoleon could not tolerate another
power in his land, but nor could he deprive the people of the comfort
they needed from their religion. The government decision, supported
by Napoleon, to re-open the churches and re-institute Sunday worship was hugely popular. How could post-revolutionary France
convince a Pope of the new attitude to religion in France, persuade
him to accept the loss of feudal lands, whilst still wanting him in
the hearts of the majority of the French population, mostly devout
Roman Catholics?

The status of the Catholic Church was one of the main unsettled reforms
of the Revolution. In particular, vast amounts of Church-owned lands

had been sold by the State, and the new owners were wary of investing further if the Church's claims might soon be restored.

Napoleon officially recognized Catholicism as the religion of the majority of Frenchmen (which pleased the Pope), but supported the idea of liberty of worship (which did not).

There were many contradictions here. The demands of the Revolution and the increasing power of Napoleon both represented anti-Papal forces; certainly Napoleon, brought up in a strictly Catholic environment, resented the power of the Papacy. He had seen the dangers of religious strife in Corsica, in Italy and in Egypt, and was critical of what he saw as the negative influence of Catholicism. After the Italian Wars, Napoleon wanted to make peace treaties with Rome as with other participants in his conflicts. The Pope refused, hoping that the Austrians would win, but by February 1797 he was ready to come to terms, and was forced to cede Bologna, Ferrara and the Romagna, and pay a substantial indemnity. Napoleon wanted to enter Rome and depose the Pope, but was afraid of his own pro-Catholic forces at home, and realized that this might be going too far.

Napoleon had hoped that the Concordat would not be necessary, as privately he thought that the huge loss of territory and the imposition of heavy taxes would mean that the archaic machinery of the Papacy would break down and save him the trouble. Naïvely, Napoleon believed that when the very elderly Pope died, that would be the end of the rule of Catholics from Rome, and there would be no more Popes. But publicly he had to express hope that the French Republic would be a true friend of Rome; and he had to bear in mind his hopes for extending his influence in Italy and Spain, deeply Catholic societies.

Despite his anti-religious feelings, Napoleon was alert to the levers of popular support. The decision during the early years of the Revolution to erase Sunday from the calendar was clearly unpopular. As we have seen, the months of the year had been given new names, and the years were no longer reckoned from the birth of Christ. This had upset many. Napoleon had to be seen to support the Revolution, but he realized the value of religion in bringing order to society. He knew that the mass of French people wanted to follow their faith. He wanted to reconcile differences, and therefore had to work things out with the Pope. So he prepared to re-open the churches, which the Revolutionaries had closed during 1789–90. But this alone was not enough.

Napoleon saw that the Revolution had failed in terms of establishing a clear religious policy. The churches had been closed and the Church lands nationalized in 1789, and bishops and other members of the clergy were now in the pay of the State and had to be elected (they were no longer appointed by the Pope). After the fall of Robespierre, the official policy of the administration of France was a complete separation of Church and State, and tolerance of other religious sects was declared. But it was still a very messy and unclear situation.

In 1799 more than 9,000 priests had been deported from France by the Directory. There had been violence against the Church, especially with claims of corruption amongst the clergy, but many purists were against the Church being made subservient to the State.

Napoleon thus saw the political advantages of a concordat, of doing a deal with Rome. Not only would he disassociate Catholicism from Royalism, he would also be able to reassure those who had bought the ex-Church lands that they would not lose their newly acquired assets. He could thereby strengthen French influence in Catholic countries – such as Italy, Belgium and the Rhine – offsetting possible rival and domestic influences. The loyalty to Napoleon in Catholic areas, such as Warsaw, was unimpaired by the Concordat. One of his especially manipulative moves was to accuse Pope Pius VII of being not only a discredited Royalist but also of being a discredited Jacobin, in his search for reasons for perpetuating his attack on the Church. The Concordat could also preserve Napoleon's power in the countryside of France.

In July 1801, when agreement was reached after long and hard bargaining, the nature of the compromise deal became apparent, in four particular ways. First, the Concordat recognized Catholicism as the religion of most Frenchmen – but not as the 'established' or the 'dominant' religion in the wording the Pope wanted. Second, public worship was allowed but only when conforming to strict police regulations. Third – and most controversially – all the bishops had to resign and new ones would be appointed. The idea was that the First Consul could nominate the bishops and the Pope would then institute them, especially as the French government would pay their salaries, but the Pope hung onto the small amount of power he had left and refused to do the instituting required, pressing to call clerical pay 'endowments' rather than 'salaries'. Fourth, Napoleon insisted that the nationalization of the Church lands was irrevocable, whilst the Pope was refusing – unsuccessfully – to renounce the Church lands in France. Napoleon's insistence on freedom of religious practice also annoyed the Pope, although in practice Catholicism was by far the religion of choice for most people.

Many observers saw the Concordat as a way of Napoleon acquiring domination over the Church, and thereby over the people. This was seen as part of a trend towards a lack of freedom in France introduced by Napoleon, and part of Napoleon's view of the supremacy of the State and himself as leader. He counter-claimed that he was reinforcing the primacy of the State over the Church, one of the aims of the Revolution, and resistance was mostly due to clerical ambition, corruption and the medieval backwardness of the Church. Napoleon's anti-feudalism stand here was a way of further consolidating his position against the Church.

As an agnostic if not an atheist, Napoleon was realistic enough to realize that he would be opposed by politicians and generals in creating the Concordat – and, of course, by the émigrés from the Revolution who may at first have been religious sceptics but who had become more religious in exile, especially those in non-Catholic lands such as England. There was no spiritual or religious basis for the dispute between Napoleon and the Pope: from Napoleon's point of view, it was purely political. Religious exiles had already remarked on the profound moral indifference of Napoleon which, they pointed out, was not seen as typical of a real Frenchman. A Corsican, perhaps, but not a Frenchman.

The stipends of the clergy were to be paid by the French state in a law of April 1802. The Pope was glad of the cash for the clergy, but effectively lost control of his priests in France this way. The government paying the wages of the priests in effect made them State employees. The Pope wanted these payments to be called 'endowments' but Napoleon insisted that they were 'salaries'. The Pope wanted to keep his power of appointing clergy; Napoleon insisted that they would be elected. After stripping him of much of his power, Napoleon still wanted the Pope to be present at his coronation – and His Holiness felt he had little choice but to attend, especially given that France was one of the largest Catholic countries.

One important area of concern that Napoleon did not foresee was the reaction from many of the generals, who carried on supporting the Pope. Meanwhile many politicians abused the Concordat for their own aims. Napoleon's minister Talleyrand, who had been a bishop and had been involved in dis-establishing the Church during the Revolution, disapproved of re-establishing it, especially as he wanted priests to be able to marry (including himself). But after the Peace of Amiens Napoleon had much stronger popular support, and was less worried by opposition in what he saw as isolated quarters.

Inspite of the opposition to the Concordat in many areas, it achieved Napoleon's objectives of consolidating his power as he was able to use the success of his negotiations and ability to alienate the opposition to strengthen his position. Thirty-eight of the ninety-three bishops refused to resign or recognize the Concordat, the Pope refused to institute the

twelve bishops nominated by Napoleon because they were seen as coming from the revolutionary period; some bishops expelled their local
clergy; and the Pope kept saying that the way the Concordat was passed
into law was a breach of faith. In spite of this, or even because of it,
Napoleon's popularity in the country rose to a height. Many people must
have felt divided loyalties between their support of the Church and the
exciting independence of the new populist State. France was becoming
great under Napoleon. Even the Pope had to make terms with him!

But Napoleon's was a pyrrhic victory, gained without the Pope's full
approval. It would not be accurate to claim that Napoleon dominated
the Pope, who was not necessarily the weak character Napoleon assumed
him to be, or a petty sovereign who could be bullied.

Relations between Napoleon and the Pope continued to deteriorate,
especially when Napoleon insisted on using the title *Emperor* of Rome
(and was to call his son *King* of Rome), although he could allow the
Pope to be called *Sovereign* of Rome. Napoleon still wanted support
from the Pope against his enemies, and admitted he made a mistake in
arresting him in 1809 and offered him two million francs a year in com-
pensation. The Pope always had the trump card of excommunicating his
aggressors, although he never dared to excommunicate Napoleon specifically. The Pope still had support inside France, and when the Council
met in June 1811, two-thirds of the members refused to act in filling 27
vacancies sees without the support of the Pope.

This became an excuse for Napoleon to dissolve the Legislative Council
of France and, with agreement from a bare majority of the bishops, carried on enforcing the Concordat throughout the empire. In asserting his
position contrary to the Pope, Napoleon was taking a considerable risk – which
way would the people go? The opposition of the Council to Napoleon
had been supported by both diehard and lukewarm Catholics, who
criticized the Pope for both being on the one hand too co-operative with
Napoleon, and on the other hand standing in the way of progress and the
Revolution.

Yet overall, the Concordat of 1802 was seen as a triumph for Napoleon,
and he used this and the peace of Amiens between France, England
and Russia to extend his term as First Consul to First Consul for Life.
Although in contradiction with the constitution of the revolutionary
year VIII, which he had helped introduce with the Brumaire, Napoleon
forced the Senate to expel opposition members from the Tribunate and
the legislative body. The Senate had already suggested an extension to
10 years, but Napoleon held a plebiscite, in which three and a half million people voted in favour, with only 8,000 dissenting. He was to use

this new form of elected power to great effect in becoming Emperor, as discussed in the next chapter.

Many observers inside and outside of France saw the Concordat as evidence of the young First Consul's statesmanlike wisdom increasing the power of the State. Now a Frenchman could pray to his God only with the permission of the State. Napoleon considered that the 40,000 priests now in his pay would support him, especially from possible pro-Papacy attacks from the conservative generals. Napoleon also claimed that he was carrying on the religion of his fathers by reopening the churches and providing continuity, but his official tolerance of other faiths was criticized by extreme Catholics.

Yet Napoleon, ever the opportunist, saw the practical advantages. He could get rid of a tiresome counter-revolutionary element in the non-supportive clergy and émigré critics, and he could support a new class of landowners and newly-rich.

Napoleon made sure that the Church in France was subject to strict government regulation and tried to control it as much as possible. His relationship with the Church remained strained as a result, especially when in 1809–14 he imprisoned the Pope in Savoy. But the Concordat has been accepted by successive French regimes, and many see it as an admirable move in the creation of a modern, secular society, creating the important political distinction between Church and State.

When Napoleon found himself in difficulties, one of his first reactions was to make friends with the Pope again. After the Retreat from Moscow, Napoleon tried to reopen dialogues with the Pope, and after he was cornered at Leipzig he offered to restore the Papal States without conditions. Pius was to re-enter Rome immediately after Napoleon's first abdication. Finally, when Napoleon was in exile on St Helena, the Pope was decent enough to ask for concessions and freedoms for him, a plea ignored by the Prince Regent of England.

Reflections on leadership and power

- Napoleon could never share power willingly, he always had to have the upper hand, and would manipulate to achieve this.
- His unwillingness to share power was part of his feeling of vulnerability – he was envious of the power base enjoyed by the other 'real' monarchs of Europe.

(Continued)

(Continued)

- His pursuit of constant war meant that he could never share power with other national leaders – he was temporarily an ally or permanently an enemy.

- Other national leaders were fearful of Napoleon's ability to stir up more revolutions in their countries, and could never trust him.

- The associates with whom he interacted were rarely equal partners of Napoleon or equal partners among themselves. They were more likely to be used as tools or otherwise manipulated, and were often on their guard.

Manipulation, less coercive as a power mode and more subtle, ensures action and discussion that fit within accepted boundaries. The manipulator can shape the anticipated results by using rules, bias, networking and positioning. Setting an agenda implies shaping the issues to be discussed, and ensures that other issues do not arise. Assumptions are then inserted into decision-making frameworks without people realizing it.

The leaders of France after Brumaire – and Napoleon was not in sole control at this point – were faced with three difficult issues in the relationship between the people of France and the Papacy. First, the separation of the concept of Catholicism from the concept of Royalism, so that a republic without a traditional monarch could still administer, lead and manage the people's faith. This can be seen as a tall order for a regime, dominated by men like Napoleon who were increasingly disillusioned with religion, or like Talleyrand for whom religion was a tool. Napoleon was probably an atheist and at most only paid lip service to the need to have a faith. In exile on St Helena many years later and reflecting on his career, he thought he was better off for being a non-believer.

Second, there were practical matters at stake here too. As we have seen, the new post-revolutionary owners of former Church lands were afraid of losing them. Taking lands from the church and redistributing them was part of the revolutionary drive against feudalism, an attack on established wealth in France and an important material gain from a revolution that still faced opposition from the Papacy.

Third, Napoleon felt it necessary to keep the Bishops on his side as 'moral prefects' in the countryside, being his eyes and ears amongst the rural masses. These church leaders were useful, but he must distance them from the old monarchy and the Papacy and now use them and the village priests to help to keep the political order of his regime in the vast swathes of countryside. Napoleon had heard reports that most of the peasants in France were not influenced by revolutionary propaganda, but remained attached to their priests. So he had set himself the task of coming to terms with the Pope to get everyone on his side – in the meantime, to make the priests subject to his own patronage.

So, when Napoleon was appointed First Consul he took upon himself the task of undertaking a series of reforms – apparently to preserve the gains of the Revolution, to improve stability in France – and effectively to ensure his personal control. The *Code Civil*, later known as the *Code Napoleon*, is often cited as an example of such a reform, and another was the Concordat.

As Napoleon argued at the time (in a letter to Roederer, 1800), 'society cannot exist without inequality of wealth, and inequality of wealth cannot exist without religion. When a man is dying of hunger beside someone who has abundance, he cannot accept such a difference unless there is an authority telling him, "God wishes it thus. There must be poor and rich in this world, but afterwards, and for all eternity, the lots will be different"' (Cronin, 1971: 260).

Many observers, contemporary and later, noticed this ability to manipulate competing interest groups. For example, the Treaty of Campo Formio of October 1797, in which peace was arranged between Austria and France, included a number of secret clauses that were to sow the seeds of future discord.

Napoleon became less and less of a team player as he gained more and more power, and was increasingly an individualist. There were three potential sources of partnerships for co-operation for him, but in most cases Napoleon preferred to manipulate rather than co-operate. He could have worked more closely with other monarchs or country leaders, fellow generals and military leaders, and his family members. With other monarchs of Europe he was always the parvenu, the outsider, the pretender. The Pope, the Emperors of Austria and Prussia, the Tsar of Russia, the King of England – they could never be partners, but were mostly enemies or temporary allies at best, and rejected Napoleon's overtures of friendship. His marshals and generals, though some of his earliest associates, were rarely consulted even on military matters. Some had betrayed his trust and had become political adversaries. Anyone threatening Napoleon's power base had to be contained and stopped. He was also no team player with his family members, or even with his mother. He had to manipulate them all and bribe them just as with his other associates and, like other potential partners around him, they supported him when he was winning but were quick to desert him in defeat.

As we have seen, the crowned heads of Europe were against Napoleon in Europe. The traditional and established monarchs always saw him as an upstart. The only way he could survive was by playing them off against each other. Napoleon was thus always isolated, and could never avoid being a loner when it came to sharing power willingly. He was envious of the inherited legitimacy enjoyed by the other monarchs of Europe, but his constant involvement in war meant that they could never trust him – even when temporarily an ally he represented a permanent enmity, and sometimes a mixture of both.

The monarchs of Europe for their part constantly feared Napoleon's ability to stir up popular discontent amongst their populations, and invested heavily in demonizing him. But they were by no means a united force, and Napoleon was often able to manage them by changing sides and offering tactical advantages one over another. Those of his close associates with whom he interacted were rarely confidants or equals but tools to be used – as in the case of other military leaders, such as mar-shals and generals – or family members whom he felt obliged to support, and this tendency to use people for his own ends increased in the last decade of his career.

Manipulation helped ensure Napoleon's control over apparent and potential members of his inner sanctum of power. Napoleon's early experience of camaraderie as a soldier was perhaps always coloured by his outsider status; he was never comfortable as a member of any clique. As a general and ruler he demanded unconditional obedience and total support.

Indeed, his patronage was often given to those whose loyalty was their chief recommendation. This is revealed in his advice to his much-liked stepson Eugène de Beauharnais, the son of Josephine, when appointed viceroy of Italy: 'our subjects in Italy are naturally more dissembling than the citizens of France. Do not accord your entire confidence to anyone ... speak as little as possible, for your education has not been sufficiently thorough to allow you to indulge in discussions. Learn how to listen. Show such esteem for the nation you govern as is appropriate, particularly as you accumulate reasons for esteeming it less. A time will come when you realize that there is very little difference between one people and another' (Gallo, 1997a: 268).

The term 'manipulation' at root means 'to move and mould with the hands, a way to craft and shape opportunities'. In a more straightforward way, a military commander is authorized to manipulate his troops and resources. Generally, it is more effective if the troops are engaged and enthusiastic and understand the purposes and plans of which they are part, so rhetorical devices by which this persuasion takes place become a necessary practice. Articulating a purpose, establishing what we now call a vision and mission, are similarly important foundations for manipulation. Setting objectives is never a once-and-for-all job, so there are many variations in any complex enterprise with conflicting priorities and interests.

Anyone who wants to get things done must constantly be reaffirming specific priorities, claiming attention and diverting people's interests from other distractions. A key resource for manipulation is knowledge and information, awareness of timing, controlling who gets to know what and who does not. Transparency as a concept is much vaunted, but is always a political issue. Absolute transparency would mean that there are no secrets between people, and therefore fewer manipulative opportunities for those who hold those secrets.

The control of information is crucial in any kind of commercial context, and bargaining over prices always depends on inequalities of information. The manipulation of markets is a function of secrets, but also of monopoly, collusion, scale effects and regulatory capture. Thus manipulation is about far more than inter-personal relations or group competition; it is built into the normal practices of business and government. But being manipulated is quite different to being the manipulator. To be used for others' purposes, even with consent, is usually experienced as shameful and belittling. But more often, especially in politics, everyone is in the same game, both manipulator and manipulated; the only way to avoid this is to become the autocrat.

Yet Napoleon famously remained susceptible to Josephine's manipulations. She could almost always get around him with tears of seduction; and even when he was regularly and often sleeping with other women, he would come to her for relaxation and acceptance; perhaps, in the later years, this was the only relationship that he did not feel the need to control.

In managing the nation, Napoleon well understood the challenges of knowing what was going on and using the power of information, establishing parallel police forces to spy on each other as well as the rest of the population; and like all dictators he ensured that neither police force ever knew what the other was reporting. Keeping everyone around him in a constant state of insecurity, Napoleon could argue, why should they have security when I have so little myself?

Napoleon had to manoeuvre himself with care in relation to the Catholic Church. It was one of the more contentious and impactful outcomes of the Revolution that it had been decided to seize, purchase and sell vast tracts of land owned by the Church in an agricultural country – when land was the key to wealth in eighteenth-century France. It was understandable that as Napoleon appeared to settle into a familiar hierarchical regime and sought legitimacy from ancient institutions, the Pope tried to bargain for the Church's land. Napoleon was adamant that there would be no turning back on this departure from feudalism, but he held open the possibility as one of the means for bargaining. When it came down to it, the Pope could not be persuaded by force alone to bless Napoleon's marriage and coronation; and this blessing was a crucial element in Napoleon's manipulation of popular approval.

But it would be wrong to think that Napoleon, in a one-sided way, manipulated his ministers, the crowned heads of Europe, his generals and his family members – because he was equally manipulated by them. Talleyrand, his foreign minister, is a prime example, manoeuvring himself through many positions of power, never seeking supreme office but always in positions of influence. A long-lived survivor, he claimed in his memoirs that he never deserted a cause until it had itself deserted the interests of France – a contestable claim, but perhaps defensible.

Questions on leadership and power

Do you tend to make treaties and alliances? Are you comfortable in a pluralistic melee of competing interests or do you prefer to keep all power in your own hands? Do you use the manipulative means you have to achieve your objectives?

- Do you share power willingly, or do you always have to be in charge and safeguard your power from others?

- Would you never have a secret agenda, and tend to put all your cards on the table?

- When power and influence are distributed amongst competing parties, does this make you feel vulnerable or stronger?

- Are you envious of the power enjoyed by other leaders you see around you, or happy with your lot?

- What is your overall strategy for your career – and how does this affect the way you think about and use power?

- Are other leaders fearful of your ability to wield power even over their people? Can you influence people who do not report directly to you?

- Do you work with certain people due to a sense of obligation – you could not get rid of them even if you wanted to – and tolerate some unreliability and incompetence?

- Do you feel yourself being manipulative to get what you want, or do you refuse to tolerate 'playing games' and 'office politics'?

- Do you feel manipulated, used for the benefit of others? And if so, is it a fair exchange for the benefits you receive?

FEAR

Dealing with the opposition, 1803–04: the use and abuse of being brutal and uncompromising in securing a power base

Conquest has made me what I am. Only conquest can preserve me.

Napoleon, 1799

These Royalists mustn't labour under any illusions! They are the ones coming over to the government's side, not the government coming over to them!

Napoleon, 1800

I do not regret acting as I did towards the duc d'Enghien. Only thus would I remove all doubts as to my real intention, and destroy the hopes of the Bourbonists.

Napoleon, 1804

So he is also nothing more than an ordinary man? Now he will trample on the rights of mankind and indulge only his own ambition; from now on he will make himself superior to all others and become a tyrant.

Beethoven, the composer, on hearing about the execution of d'Enghien and the proclamation of the Empire, late 1804

There has recently been a total change in the methods of Napoleon: he seems to think that he has reached a point where moderation is a useless obstacle.

Observed by Meternich, the Austrian foreign minister,
after Tilsit, 1807

The aura which all about him manifestly feel is inconceivable to those who are not familiar with the excesses and extravagances of a man possessed with absolute power and actuated by violent and unmanageable passions.

Napoleon's minister to the United States, 1808

In this world there are only two alternatives – to command or to obey.

Napoleon to aide, December 1812

Controlling his power base, holding onto power – this became Napoleon's obsession. He developed a need to know everything that was going on, to silence opposition, and to ensure complete obedience. The use of fear to gain and keep power helped him manage any threats to his increasingly dominant position. As First Consul, Napoleon faced several assassination attempts. He dealt with 'pretenders to the throne' in a direct and uncompromising way, sending out a message of fear to any opponents. This also involved managing the media, to dissuade anyone from such attempts at seizing power for fear of the consequences. Napoleon always maintained a tight censorship of the press – not least for military security – and there were only four newspapers in Paris by 1811, one for each department of the government. All were government controlled; Napoleon himself edited *le Moniteur* and wrote many of the articles himself.

Napoleon was able to strike fear into the hearts of his opposition and win the obedience of many of his followers as a result, but this also reduced their willingness to give him honest feedback. The episode encapsulating this new phase of his leadership, the subject of this chapter, was his deliberate crackdown on potential successors to the Bourbon monarchy. This was the framing and execution of the nearest and most convenient suspect, the duc d'Enghien. It was clearly an example of the use of fear '*pour encourager les autres*' (Voltaire). There are few such blatant examples, but few were needed: fear of the consequences of rebellion quickly becomes an inner state of being in any effective dictatorship.

During the Consulate there were a number of opposition movements to Napoleon's rule – some calling for a military dictatorship, some calling for more radical republicanism, and other groups plotting the return of the Bourbon monarchy. Although the first two causes inspired more direct attacks, it was the latter that bore the brunt of Napoleon's reaction and retaliation. Prominent among these was a plot suspected to be led by the duc d'Enghien, a minor Bourbon noble who became the unfortunate focus of Napoleon's attention.

Throughout the post-revolutionary period it was assumed in many quarters that somewhere there would always be a Bourbon prince waiting for his chance when the Revolution collapsed. The diaspora of pro-Royalists would rally to support him. It was well-known that the English government was supporting Royalists in France who were planning to kidnap or assassinate Napoleon, which became an issue of increasing concern for him, pushing him to a greater use of fear as a deterrent. One assassination plot came close to succeeding, on Christmas Eve 1800. Napoleon, Josephine and her daughter Hortense set off to go to the opera, and ordered their carriages. Running late for the show at 8 p.m., Josephine's carriage was a few minutes behind Napoleon's as she rushed to get ready. An explosion went off but was misdirected and occurred between the two carriages, so the occupants were uninjured. Yet entire houses were destroyed, nine people died and 26 were injured. Napoleon was shocked and angry: 'For such an atrocious crime we must have vengeance like a thunder-bolt; blood must flow; we must shoot as many guilty men as there have been victims'. But the ringleaders were safe in England – protected by the émigré Bourbon Comte d'Artois. English money was used for funding assassins and conspirators especially after the declaration of war again in May 1803, helped by a network of Royalist agents in France from the coast to Paris to help the conspirators travel safely to the capital.

Underground pro-Royalist activity continued despite the peace of Amiens for 1802–03, which the English cynically thought was unlikely to last long, given Napoleon's track record of fomenting constant military conquest.

It was widely rumoured in Paris that a secret army, under orders from London for the restoration of Bourbons, had recently returned to France. They had been encouraged by Napoleon's amnesty (directed at trying to win over opponents of his regime in the West of France and the 40,000 Royalists living overseas) that if they laid down their arms, they could come home. Napoleon violently turned against his former attitude of rather naïve forgiveness as the émigré opponents were spurred to greater action to bring down his administration for their own benefit.

There was considerable speculation about which member of the Bourbon aristocracy was proposed by the Royalists. Amongst these was the Comte d'Artois in London, who was clearly financing and assisting in a number of plots. There was certainly evidence of several conspiracies against Napoleon in the summer of 1803, actively reported by Fouché. D'Artois himself did not return to France, so Fouché pointed to a new candidate for Napoleon's retribution. Louis Antonie, duc d'Enghien, the 31-year-old grandson of the Prince de Condé, had led corps of émigrés in the Prussian invasion of France in the Valmy campaign of 1792 near Strasbourg, and he still lived near the French border. Evidence of his involvement was slim and circumstantial, but he was easier to reach for the security services and could be abducted without difficulty.

Fouché had developed a network of agents – many of whom were double agents – who suggested that in the event of a continental war across Europe, the duc d'Enghien (with his famous Condé eagle nose) was poised to lead an émigré force into Alsace. An exiled French general and an English colonel were meanwhile in close touch with d'Enghien, according to Fouché's spies.

Napoleon was thus encouraged to assume that this must be the Bourbon prince waiting for his moment to strike, and that he should be seized immediately. This would mean violating the territory of Baden (where d'Enghien was based, near Strasbourg) but it was more accessible than England, at least. As a French subject d'Enghein was in any case liable to French law. So the Bourbon Prince was rapidly hustled to Paris on a series of rapidly created charges.

However, it was soon realized by many of Napoleon's entourage that actually d'Enghien probably wasn't part of a plot to unseat and kill the First Consul. The émigré Frenchman whom d'Enghien was with was apparently harmless and had no military record of note; the 'English' Colonel was actually a German – not Smith but Schmidt. Yet Napoleon had gone too far down the track, and was determined to make someone pay for his anxiety, and he needed a *vendetta* victim.

There was some evidence against d'Enghien: he had certainly signed a pledge in 'implacable opposition to the hated Bonaparte' and was probably in English pay, but so were many hundreds of potential supporters of a return to the Bourbons. In a meeting of his ministers and advisers led by the First Consul, it was decided that d'Enghien should be tried by a military commission. Talleyrand and Fouché were in favour, and able to overcome the opposition of the other consuls. At 1 a.m. on 21 March 1804, d'Enghien appeared before the military commission in the prison of Vincennes. He stated he had received 4,200 guineas a year to combat a government 'to which his birth had made him hostile'. He was found guilty against the law of conspiracy by 'inciting civil war against lawful authority'. By 2.30 a.m. he had been shot by firing squad. General Savary, head of the *Gendarmerie d'Elite,* backed by Fouché, was there to overawe the military commission and make sure the execution went ahead. D'Enghien had asked for an interview with Napoleon, but this was refused (Markham, 1963: 111).

The enormity of the implications of this decision did not go unnoticed at the time. One observer noted: 'this judicial murder did immense moral harm to the reputation which Napoleon had enjoyed during the Consulate as the hero-statesman' (Markham, 1963: 111). The composer Beethoven, in a rage on hearing the news, struck out the dedication of the *Eroica* symphony to Napoleon. Napoleon was seen as transitioning from admired reformer to feared autocrat. In France only Chateaubriand had the courage and principles to resign his official post in protest on the issue, but many more felt the same. The Russian court formally protested, and Talleyrand responded with a tactless reference to Tsar Paul's assassination. Napoleon had already concluded that Russia would join England as soon as the opportunity arose. Meanwhile, the Duke of Baden was too intimidated by Napoleon to formally complain. Louis XVIII, on his accession in 1814 and 1815, did not make an enquiry into the case, especially as it may indeed have uncovered the complicity of the Comte d'Artois in various plots against the First Consul. It could have been that the English government supported such plots to assassinate Napoleon, although it was always denied. In any case, Talleyrand destroyed all the documents just before the Bourbon restoration, so that he could say in his memoirs that he had tried to save d'Enghien from execution.

Commentators at the time reflected that in France it was widely seen as unnecessary to execute d'Enghien, if the purpose was just to confirm that there had been an assassination conspiracy. This had already been demonstrated by rounding up the ring-leaders. French public opinion wavered. Napoleon was excused by many on the grounds that he must have realized that d'Enghien was harmless, and there had been a mistake. D'Enghien was not guilty, and was not dangerous, but it was alarming that Napoleon would not calmly reconsider the charges. He refused to listen to Josephine's pleas for clemency, accusing her of wanting to see him murdered. Some observers commented that Napoleon had been turned from good to evil and moderation to violence by the shock of the Royalist assassination attempts – not necessarily excusing him but trying to identify the causes of his brutality.

Court officials close to Napoleon, such as Madame de Rémusat, the wife of the Chamberlain, saw the execution as a deliberate act of statecraft, that Napoleon was convinced it was the price he must pay to assure the ex-Revolutionaries that he was on their side. By shedding Bourbon blood he became the Revolutionaries' accomplice as a regicide. He was standing up for the gains of the Revolution, trying to irrevocably prevent a restoration of the monarchy. This extreme example of retaliation had the concrete effect that Royalist plots against Napoleon stopped.

This was certainly closer to Napoleon's assessment. On his deathbed in St Helena he wrote: 'I had the duc d'Enghien arrested and tried because it was necessary to do so for the safety, interests, and the honour of the French people, at a time when the Comte d'Artois openly admitted that he had paid sixty assassins in Paris. In like circumstances, I should do so again' (Markham, 1963: 112). He did it to stop factions thriving against him, realizing he had to persecute, deport and condemn – or be assassinated.

To the majority of traditional leaders in Europe, the behaviour of Napoleon in this episode confirmed him as an unpredictable, power-mad upstart and that he would never be a member of 'the club'. It was observed that Napoleon did not succeed in gaining moral acceptance by the European powers as a legitimate ruler, and that the Napoleonic wars were, like the wars of the sixteenth century and the Second World War, an ideological conflict. In the minds of Napoleon's enemies, there was a code of conduct related to treating Napoleon which they would never have applied to a legitimate monarch.

Therefore, the inherited crowned heads of Europe thought it was fair game to try to assassinate Napoleon as he wasn't a legitimate monarch. So when he crowned himself Emperor, even with the Pope's blessing, this was just part of his parvenu and adventurer style of operating. It didn't make him part of the club, despite what Napoleon had intended. Even then, it was expected by the rest of Europe that his ephemeral, home-made administration would collapse at any moment. He was never going to last.

The execution of d'Enghien was seen as Napoleon at his most controversial. Many of those who had been in favour of Napoleon or at least neutral now turned against him and did not turn back. It became a stratagem of Napoleon to try to get rid of any limitations to his power that still existed. He reacted to any kind of threat, and used the Christmas Eve 1800 attack to purge the left-wing opposition as well as the Royalists. He forced through a government statement labelling 130 Republicans as terrorists, especially those who had resisted his coup at Brumaire. Many were imprisoned or deported. Even when Fouché showed that it had been Royalists and not Republicans behind the Christmas Eve attack, the crack-down continued and more prisoners were guillotined. This brutal retaliation was led by Napoleon, but there was now at least some political support for a repressive state.

From the time of the execution onwards, it was observed that Napoleon was increasingly prone to emotional violence and egoism. He had faced life-threatening danger in war, but the assassination attempts were personal and seem to have shaken him more, so he became prone to the kind of self-centred paranoia that characterizes so many autocrats. Some said that he now saw himself as above the law, as if his personal interests were indistinguishable from those of the State or the common good. He appeared to have few feelings of sympathy, admiration or pity, and was surrounded by servants and instruments, not collaborators or partners. To ensure that everyone trembled at the master, there would always be war from now on. Observers commented that Napoleon lost respect for common moral values and a sense of moderation, becoming heartless and stopping at nothing to achieve his ends.

This phase of the Consulate was marked by much more constrained political freedoms which many people accepted out of a mixture of fear and desire for a more settled order and, for some, the enjoyment of privilege derived from Napoleon's patronage. At the same time, he was laying the foundations for his own imperial, monarchical regime.

Reflections on leadership and power

- Napoleon became increasingly paranoid through fear of assassination attempts.

- He thought that all the gains of the Revolution would be lost if the assassins succeeded.

- As a result he closely managed all sources of power and influence in France, developing a network of informants and spies and closing down any oppositional newspapers to enable him to dominate the media.

- The execution of a potential 'pretender' would demonstrate the fearful consequences of any opposition.

- So he made an example of the execution of the duc d'Enghien.

Napoleon has been criticized for allowing himself to be surrounded by 'yes'-men, but it is common for people working closely with senior leaders to be economical with the truth, flatter them, and even become blatant liars. When followers are fearful and scared by a strong leader in a hierarchical organization – such as when working daily with Napoleon, in his army or government – they told him what they thought he wanted to hear.

Many of Napoleon's followers, not of high social-status, were unfamiliar with positions of power and lacked the confidence to act beyond the structures of military command. In organizations where dissenters are dismissed and there is constant pressure to perform, followers are likely to experience fear, uncertainty and doubt – and are likely to become dependent, conformist and unquestioning, whatever they might think privately to themselves.

In spite of Napoleon's almost absolute control of civil and military power in the country by the early years of the nineteenth century, he nevertheless felt insecure, and with good reason. At a time when he felt vulnerable, that his power base was not entirely secure, his anxiety was further fuelled by his growing worry about his own mortality, and that he had no declared successor – particularly that he had no son and heir. He was surely right to believe the Royalists a real threat both to himself and the more egalitarian ideals of the Revolution? But his narcissistic fantasy that could be served only by reproducing himself through hereditary succession was tragically mistaken. There could be no mercy for anyone potentially challenging the First Consul.

Yet even in a contemporary tradition of summary justice, this episode was regarded as one of the most controversial decisions ever made by Napoleon. He was influenced by his marshals and advisers, but they were divided in their views. Josephine had desperately wanted to save d'Enghien, but this might just have been out of personal sympathy for him, and fear of the violent direction in which Napoleon's personality was taking him.

It is worth considering five issues here:

1. The model of the Corsican-style *vendetta* as a response to assassination attempts when he could not bring actual perpetrators to justice.

2. Napoleon's desire to safeguard what he saw as the gains of the Revolution, as if he personally was the custodian of these gains, he surely had to be seen to be on the side of the Revolutionists by getting rid of Bourbon pretenders whenever possible.

3. To justify his acceptance of 'pressure' to accept an hereditary title, to guarantee continuity and prevent Jacobin anarchy or the retrogressive step of a Bourbon restoration.

4. Napoleon's extensive and powerful police forces were seeking to justify their existence and ingratiate themselves with their leader.

5. A threat to disgruntled politicians and military officers pushed aside by Napoleon's huge ambition.

First, this episode can be seen as having a link with Napoleon's Corsican origins. Although he disapproved of the use of *vendetta* and saw it as a barbarous custom, there were two occasions in his career when he reverted to the *vendetta* concept: the execution of d'Enghien; and the bequest in his will to the man who tried to assassinate the Duke of Wellington on his behalf. Napoleon was not an extreme bully, and could have been much tougher, evidenced by his reluctance to treat Josephine in the way that many Corsicans would have treated an unfaithful wife who brought humiliation and shame on her husband. Perhaps in Napoleon's mind the code of the Corsican *vendetta* was honoured by the execution. An attack by one member of a clan (by supporters of the Comte d'Artois) could be avenged by the death of another. D'Enghien was from the same clan, the Bourbons, and one of them had to be got rid of to make the point.

Second, Napoleon argued that the execution of d'Enghien, and the crackdown on similar opponents, safeguarded the gains of the Revolution. Napoleon argued, and many agreed, that his personal vulnerability made the Revolution vulnerable. Maintaining and defending France and her territories and therefore the start of the new order in Europe that the Revolution signalled, all depended on him personally. It was suggested by an observer that many of the beneficiaries of the Revolution who took advantage of the nationalized lands of the Church, as well as the returning émigrés protected by Napoleon, could never feel safe whilst the survival of the current regime depended solely on Napoleon's life. Many at the time believed that if he were assassinated or killed in battle, the result might be a return to the anarchy and chaos of the Jacobin era or a Bourbon restoration and a return to the much-disliked former monarchy.

Third, Napoleon had said to his journalist friend Roederer in 1801 after an earlier plot, 'if I die in four of five years, the clock will be wound up and will run. If I die before then, I don't know what will happen' (Cronin, 1971: 300). By 1804 he was widely reported as saying that the assassins would end up killing him and putting the Jacobins back in power. He was still insisting that he was the one person who embodied and personified the French Revolution.

Fourth, Napoleon argued that the execution of d'Enghien would stop further attempts on his life, and this would be strengthened by his acceptance of the title of Emperor. He was right here: such attempts ceased when he was enthroned. One of the reasons he gave for being appointed Emperor was to create a hereditary succession as the only possible solution to a comeback of the Jacobins or Royalists. The irony would appear to have been lost on Napoleon, and in any case 'Emperor' was seen as quite a different concept than 'King' and also meant including and consolidating the territorial gains of France by incorporating minor kingdoms.

Fifth, the efforts of Fouché, Napoleon's active chief of police, egged Napoleon on to sterner measures towards any opposition. Like Talleyrand, Fouché was just as manipulative as his leader. He could have been trying to make himself indispensable to Napoleon, especially as his chief was not used to taking elaborate security precautions. Fouché knew that the constant threat of assassination was wearing Napoleon down and getting on his nerves, and with encouragement from Fouché he could be driven to violent retaliation, which would play into Fouché's hands. Thus there were many arrests of Royalists in Paris at this time, 1802–04, with 19 condemned to death (eight were reprieved and sent to prison). Napoleon was reluctant to be too tough at first – he was keen on civil equality and human rights – but crackdowns were a necessary part of being a dictator and conqueror. This is the same Napoleon as the young soldier disgusted at the executions of rebels after Toulon; and the commander who ordered 200 protesters shot on the streets of Paris in 1795.

Finally, many disgruntled and marginalized officers, among them his old friend Bernadotte, wanted to replace Napoleon with a military federation. He and several others considered dressing up as Hussars and attacking Napoleon on the parade ground when they had their chance. But there was some dissent between the would-be assassins as to whether they wanted a Bourbon restoration or a military dictatorship? And who would be the new dictator?

Thus the duc d'Enghien episode was seen by many as a watershed in Napoleon's career. Romantics and scholars who saw Napoleon as a different brand of leader lost faith in him when he used retribution to isolate and punish suspected claimants to his throne. Napoleon's increasing paranoia meant that he closely managed and controlled all the sources of power and influence in the Empire, including developing not just one but at least two networks of informants and spies, and closing down any oppositional newspapers. From being focused on inspirational leadership with his soldiers he moved towards a stronger emphasis on detailed day-to-day management.

The advantages of the close management of a power base can mean fewer nasty surprises, awareness of the availability of resources and a keen idea of what is going on; but tight management (especially that driven by fear) as well as an all-encompassing leadership and management role by one person can be exhausting and all-consuming for the individual concerned.

The use of fear as a tool of management – a subtle, coercive power – can encourage passive, blind obedience, and mediocrity, as a fear of the consequences of being outspoken can prevent honest feedback, original thinking and even just exceptional competence.

Yet it has been suggested that sometimes Napoleon was not ruthless enough. He seemed to tolerate the intrigues of colleagues who let him down, such as Bernadotte, Fouché, Talleyrand and Murat. He responded to the ingratitude of his defaulting followers with a stoical shrug. In his use of coercive power he still protected his family and marshals; he was callous but not cruel, an autocrat but not a totalitarian dictator. He was not vindictive to those who were close and loyal to him, even if they were incompetent. He did not come over as particularly intimidating. 'Nabot a peur' (the dwarf is afraid), was shown on posters across Paris, a clever anagram of Buonaparte (the Corsican spelling of Bonaparte), as a reaction to his backlash against perceived opponents. Others protested that 'ce fol empire ne durera pas son an' (this crazy empire won't last a year). During the period of the threat of invasion of England, mothers nursing their babies said 'Be quiet or Boney will get you' – but it is questionable how real the threat of invasion was felt. And Napoleon was still forced to justify his actions. When Tsar Alexander criticized his removal and execution of d'Enghien, Napoleon retorted in anger that Alexander, who had his father strangled, did not have the right to teach him lessons in behaviour. It might be suggested that if Napoleon was truly terrifying, no one would dare to confront him.

In one sense fear was never absent from Napoleon's daily life, although he was incredibly brave and fearless in battle. He was constantly active and on edge in preserving his position, forcing his enemies to reveal themselves and was quick to destroy them, but was he really paranoid? Although some biographers see him that way, he was probably no more prone to paranoia than anyone else in that position.

Yet in a regime in which every display of opposition is potentially fatal, opposition to Napoleon was driven more and more underground, and became more desperate, so that only the assassination of Napoleon would make a difference. Any one of the attempts could have been successful. Autocratic rulers must be constantly alert to both opportunistic and concerted movements to remove them from power. A pervasive culture of fear may be successful in dissuading many people from open disagreement, but only with constant and rigorous surveillance and enforcement can a leader control whole populations.

When military regimes carry over to a civilian sphere, political disagreement is seen as insubordination or even treachery. In a military setting, the line of command is of extreme importance, where the hierarchy must be preserved. Napoleon put together a *levée en masse*, an amateur army, which was not held together by training or long tradition but by fear, and the physical need to be fed and clothed. Pitched against the Austrians, well equipped and well trained, the French soldiers had little alternative but to obey in battle and celebrate their solidarity in victory.

By 1804 Napoleon had reached a dominant position. It is perhaps remarkable that there was not more competition from others to achieve military successes, and to challenge the ongoing concentration of power in the Consulate and Empire. In the early days of the Revolution many had participated in different political factions, and the Directory and Councils were large and diverse. The Consulate was a radical departure from the more distributed leadership of the past. Formed in the crucible of the coup d'état of Brumaire, this concentration of power inevitably faced opposition from an outlawed political class now habituated to political influence: they had to be dealt with severely and uncompromisingly for the regime to survive.

This is understood more clearly when seen in the context of an almost universal experience of dislocation, not just punctuated by sudden, sharp fear but where fear was ubiquitous, a below-the-surface fearfulness. The social order of centuries had broken down, the Church had been dis-established, underground rebellions were breaking out and an overall climate of chaos and confusion pervaded the scene. A young man approaching puberty at the time of the Revolution would now be in his early 20s and would be called up to fight. Boys as young as 15, once seen as 'too puny to carry a musket', were conscripted. The energy of society was directed to war or the threat of war. No one had any confidence that tomorrow would be the same as today. There was constant radical change and uncertainty.

Napoleon felt he had to use coercive power to avoid appearing weak, and to provide a measure of certainty at the centre of this confusion. To bolster his strength, though, he often made others feel weak instead. His power base was always fragile, so he always had to make others feel that something might be done to them if they did the wrong thing. If he took a miss-step he knew he was doomed. He was very conscious of this, and felt the need to make others feel like this too.

The German philosopher Nietzsche saw Napoleon as flawed by his inhumanity, but the 'higher man' was inherently dangerous by definition and acted 'whatever the cost in men' as a noble leader will accept the sacrifice of others as part of his mission. Napoleon was not sadistic or cruel, just callous and indifferent – his mission was not halted by compassion or mercy. According to Nietzsche, the power and vitality of his soul made Napoleon great, despite his use of fear, as he symbolized the hopes and dreams of the nineteenth century more than any other single leader.

Questions on leadership and power

Should you be a carefully controlling manager as well as an inspirational leader? How do you effectively manage your power base? Instilling fear is part of the mix, when moderation might fail.

- Do you find yourself closely managing sources of power and influence in your organization, developing a network of informants about what's happening, enabling you to dominate the information flows? Or is this not of interest to you and sounds obsessive?

- Is there any policy or achievement you have created that might be lost if you lost your job? That no-one else could continue?

- Do you feel you need to spread the word about the fearful consequences of any opposition to your leadership? Or this is not the way you choose to operate?

- Do you notice in yourself an increasing paranoia that you might lose your job or something else precious to you? Or does this not worry you?

- Have you ever made an example of a potentially difficult employee to make a point?

- Do you see the practice of management as a way of preserving resources and increasing efficiency, rather than of control of your colleagues?

- Are you or people around you controlling themselves for fear of what might happen if they don't?

- Is failure tolerated? Are there costs to those who innovate and fail? Do all the rewards go to those who conform?

ELECTION

The Emperor by popular acclaim, 1804: cashing-in on large-scale public opinion to build up and justify power

The wish to make Napoleon emperor originated in the French people's desire to acclaim the man they considered a hero, to raise him higher and higher. The feeling increased with each [assassination] plot discovered. A Royalist agent said – 'he has only his sword, and it is a sceptre that one hands on'.

Cronin, 1971, p302

We have done more than we hoped to do; we meant to give France a King, and we have given her an Emperor.

An imprisoned would-be assassin, 1804

By crowning himself Emperor in the presence of the Pope in Paris, he ensured recognition of his right to authority while assuming a title that would enable him to rule over a greater unit than the old Kingdom of France ... at its zenith in 1811 the French Empire stretched from Lubeck on Baltic to Gaeta, south of Rome – and included a stretch of the Dalmatian coast.

Palmer, 1962, p117

No-one can reverse the redistribution of property, and that the ancien régime *will never be restored, even if the aristocrats are returning. They do so as servants of the new order – mine.*

Napoleon, in denial, 1805

I keep throwing out anchors for my salvation into the depths of the sea.

Napoleon, facing continued isolation, 1805

Did he believe that when we have titles, honours and lands, we will kill ourselves for his sake?

Many old soldiers who turned against Napoleon, 1814

Plebiscite, or referendum, became a distinctive decision-making mechanism in the Revolution. Napoleon used it several times, and in 1804 did so again to cement his direct links with voters, reaching beyond the Paris elites. In doing so he simplified the question of governance into a single question: 'Do you want me as your Emperor?' By a huge majority, they said 'yes', and Napoleon proceeded to plan and perform a spectacular coronation, presented as a glorious expression of the will and desire of France.

In this chapter we consider how an election became the means not for wider distribution of power, but for its more intense concentration. In particular, we focus on the coronation as the ritual event that meant to embody the collective identity of all French; the expression of their decision as expressed in the plebiscites.

The coronation was to be a showy demonstration of his popularity and at the same time, his superiority. Following the negotiation of the Concordat, the peace of Amiens and the crack-down on opponents, he wanted a public demonstration that he still had the backing of the mass of Frenchmen. While he showcased his apparent popularity, behind the scenes he was rooting out opponents and consolidating his control of every branch of government. The massive showy coronation he organized was wonderfully impressive to people in need of inspiration, who wanted to lift their heads high as Frenchmen and revel in *la Gloire*, especially after the disruption of 15 years of revolution, war and economic decline. The coronation, the focus of this chapter, also promised security and stability, as the purpose of it was to sanctify the creation of a hereditary title – although war and chaos were to continue.

On 18 May 1804, Napoleon was proclaimed Emperor by the Senate, and the Constitution of the Year XII was confirmed. Millions of loyal subjects approved the proclamation by plebiscite; they deserved an ultra-grand,

showy event, a coronation better than anything the Bourbon monarchy had ever laid on. As Napoleon sat down to plan his coronation, he envisaged a ceremony mostly for the benefit of the public, so that people would see that the award of the title of Emperor established peace in France. It would discourage the Bourbons and their allies from thinking that there could ever be a restoration. It would reconcile France with the rest of Europe, because Napoleon would also be a crowned head like them; it would reconcile the old France with the new; and would wipe out any old remnants of feudalism left in Europe by associating the idea of nobility with the concept of public service.

The principle of equality was upheld in the new Napoleonic imperial regime in so far that titles were given to men without regard to their ancestry, though in fact more and more of the old noblesse were to rally to the new court after Napoleon's amnesty brought 40,000 back to France. Titles were given after recognized service to the State, and along with titles, often land and lucrative jobs in public administration. This policy made many generals rich, but led many old soldiers to prefer peace and security in which to enjoy their wealth.

To become Emperor would also cement the centralization of unitary authority. Napoleon was tolerant of opposition in private discussion, but morbidly sensitive to public opposition. His argument was that 'there is a great difference between free discussion in a country whose institutions are long established and the opposition in a country that is still unsettled', suggesting that the state of chaos and uncertainty in France and its possessions justified this policy. But he revealed his real thinking when he admitted: 'I haven't been able to understand yet what good there is in an opposition. Whatever it may say, its only result is to diminish the prestige of authority in the eyes of the people' (Markham, 1963: 99).

Various elements were combined in the coronation, reflecting its many functions. The presence of the Pope was essential to please the great mass of the people. The coronation would pay homage to history, iconography and ritual, and would confirm his legitimacy in the eyes of the people. To mark the gains of the Revolution, it would be a different style of coronation, with transparency, openness, and for all the people – not just clergy, but women and children too. But there was to be no doubt about the man of the moment, and the ultimate arrogance of Napoleon crowning himself and his wife.

Napoleon argued that 'it is the people, not God, who give crowns'. However, at the same time he thought that civil ceremonies needed religion, 'since priests are required – we might as well call in the most important, best qualified, the head priest – in other words – the Pope'. There was obviously a good deal of compromise going on here on both sides. A stunning and lavish coronation ceremony in the presence of His Holiness would be seen as a victory for France. This was something that England – the most hated enemy – could not do!

Napoleon carefully avoided accusations of hypocrisy by planning not to take communion at the coronation. He also saw to it that the Pope could absent himself at the moment when Napoleon swore to uphold freedom of worship – as the Pope could not condone this – by retreating into the sacristy and leaving the ceremony. But it was clearly politic for both Napoleon and the Pope to co-operate, focusing on an ostentatious show of unity, despite the sceptics and outright atheists present. Napoleon was too important to be turned down by anyone. The Pontiff, like many leaders of Europe, may have been biding his time until the inevitable fall of this Corsican upstart. Meanwhile, the Pope could speculate on the millions of francs that Napoleon would donate to the Church as a result of this grand gesture.

As well as celebrating the modern and new, the coronation should be firmly rooted in French historical tradition. It was widely observed at the time that Napoleon's actions were reminiscent of Charlemagne and other great leaders of the past. Indeed, Napoleon deliberately wanted to emphasize the link with Charlemagne, and made great efforts to locate Charlemagne's sword and crown and use them in the ceremony. In the end he chose to crown himself with an open crown, designed to look like Caesar's laurel leaves, but in gold, as the Romans awarded to victors. This was designed to highlight the contrast with the closed crown worn by the traditional hereditary – and degenerate – kings.

Napoleon's decision to crown himself may be seen as arrogance, or to avoid disputes, or to stop the Pope looking too powerful after the Concordat. Who else was there to crown him? The other crowned heads of Europe were mostly enemies. His own family members were unimpressive and inappropriate. He didn't trust most of his officers of state and didn't want them to look more important than him, and that also applied to the generals and marshals. There was no alternative but to crown himself.

A commission was set up to choose an imperial emblem to mark the new dynasty being created. The cock was a popular symbol of France, but it was a creature of the farmyard and seemed too weak to symbolize Napoleon. The lion was the mascot of an enemy – England. So he decided on the eagle – but not too much like that of Austria or Prussia. For his personal emblem, Napoleon wanted something ancient and unique, and decided to cover his cloak with embroideries of bees. Perhaps like Napoleon himself, they represented industry, service, fruitfulness – and a powerful sting!

Deciding on the ritual was more difficult. How, under a republic having undergone a revolution, could a monarch undergo the process of being made sacred? Napoleon knew the ceremony would be long and boring (he yawned several times) so he allowed an anointing of his brow and hands only, when there were usually nine places to be anointed. Ironically, this was to be done with olive oil and balsam, when the French kings traditionally had been anointed with holy oil brought from heaven by a dove (the phial of holy oil had been destroyed in the Revolution, coincidentally by Josephine's first husband, General Beauharnais).

Napoleon wanted to make the ceremony more inclusive and representative of the equality espoused by the Revolution. He was often regarded as a misogynist and the status of women in the economy and society made little progress during his career, but the French Republic was referred to as *la patrie*, a female noun, and the symbol of the republic was depicted as a woman. There were medieval connotations, too, in the chivalric ideals of knights performing deeds for fair ladies, so in the coronation Josephine was to be anointed and crowned too. She had been rushed through a religious marriage ceremony to Napoleon because during the revolutionary period, when all churches were closed, citizens were married in civil ceremonies only, and this was seen by the Pope as not acceptable for the coronation.

So, on 2 December 1804 Napoleon, wearing a white silk shirt, breeches, stockings, a short purple cape with Russian ermine embroidered with golden bees and a black felt hat with white plumes instead of his usual little bicorn hat, sat in his carriage and progressed to Notre Dame, accompanied by the radiant Josephine wearing a diamond bandeau. As they were slowly drawn through the streets, the crowds waved, and as they walked up the Nave and the military band played the Coronation March, the crowds shouted 'Vive l'Emperor!' Eight thousand supporters gathered in the cathedral to watch the sacring in public. Napoleon, unlike Louis XVI, had the full ceremony conducted in view of the whole congregation, trying to send a message of transparency in the new order.

The recitation of the litanies was then followed by the anointing and the first part of mass, including the blessing of the regalia: the orb, the symbol of justice, the sword and the sceptre. At that point Napoleon walked to the altar and crowned himself, to shouts of '*Vivat imperator in aeternum*' by the choir, and then he crowned Josephine. The artist David in the famous coronation painting depicted this moment, lending even more symbolic prominence to Napoleon as Emperor. Then the rituals of the three-hour ceremony continued, culminating in the oath in which Napoleon swore to maintain the integrity of the territory of the republic – at that point it included France, Belgium, Savoy, the left bank of the Rhine and Piedmont. Napoleon also swore to uphold the laws of the Concordat and freedom of worship: 'I swear to rule for the interests, happiness and glory of the people of France', Napoleon announced, and the herald shouted 'The most glorious and august Napoleon, Emperor of the French, is consecrated and enthroned!' (Cronin, 1971: 312).

What were some of the reactions after the coronation? Napoleon said he was the same as before but, despite the affectation of continuing to wear his crown through dinner that night, and insisting that Josephine did the same, he kept saying it didn't change him, and this would seem to be true. But it changed others towards him, especially with the emphasis on *la Gloire* in his coronation oath. The implication was that the Empire would expand, which it did in the next five years, and then that Empire would have to be defended. War would inevitably continue.

However popular it was among the people, the coronation did nothing to convince other monarchs of Napoleon's sovereignty over them: they were still his superiors. The coronation did not impress those for whom the observance of national laws took greater prominence. It was seen that Napoleon not only failed to observe even his own national laws, but he would make up new ones as he went along. Other European leaders did not consider Napoleon to be bound by the oath he had taken at his coronation; it was easy to say that Corsicans followed opportunities and relationships, not laws, and the coronation was just for show and part of his obsession with legitimacy.

The coronation and imperial title were not enough for Napoleon to break free from his isolation among the crowned heads of Europe, and he was even more isolated from his ministers, generals and people. He sought the semblance of legitimacy, but was nonetheless a young upstart parvenu soldier from the colonies. He was still only 35. He had been lucky on the battlefield, and was now surrounding himself with more and more trappings of power. Worst of all as far as other monarchs were concerned, he threatened more war, chaos, upheaval and economic dislocation, for France and the rest of Europe.

Reflections on leadership and power

- The use of plebiscites in France gave Napoleon huge power and helped to justify his dominant leadership.

- Napoleon liked shows of popular support – he loved the adulation of thousands.

- Show, drama, gorgeous uniforms, chivalry, huge crowds and the presence of the Pope were a way to people's hearts and built up Napoleon as a celebrity.

- People followed Napoleon (and still admire him) as 'he made France great' – and the coronation seemed to confirm and strengthen this feeling.

As we have seen, Napoleon's popularity in the country had risen to a height with the Concordat and the peace treaties, and he had used this to extend his term as First Consul to First Consul for Life. At first the authorities declared an extension of 10 years, but Napoleon (who would accept nothing less than a lifetime appointment to consolidate his power base) argued that a plebiscite should be held. If he could gain elected power, he could feel more secure, and would have facts and figures to 'prove' his popularity. The plebiscite that confirmed him as Life Consul saw three and a half million Frenchmen voting in favour, and only 8,000 dissenting, including, surprisingly, many soldiers in the army. This was seen by Napoleon as a warm-up for his election as Emperor, whereby he could increase his personal power and gain an ultimate accolade, as a crowned monarch – but carefully making the distinction that he wasn't a king. Just two years later, in that vote he had increased his support base to four million in favour, and only 3,000 against.

In April 1804, the ministers voted in favour of the principle of heredity and dynasty. It was then agreed, subject to plebiscite, that 'the Government of the Republic is entrusted to a hereditary Emperor', so that succession would stay in his family. France had been a monarchy for 14 centuries and, after the failure of successive Republican constitutions to sustain a stable government, the absence of a hereditary leader was evidently disturbing for many people.

Initially, Napoleon's ministers had agreed that if Napoleon had no son or adopted son, his brother Joseph was to be his heir. This was always going to be contentious as Napoleon didn't want any of his brothers as his heir (it would have made sibling rivalries a bit too risky), and wanted to be free to appoint his own choice of successor. He definitely needed an heir to continue the dynasty that he hoped would provide stability. He hesitated to divorce Josephine; he still had hopes that she might bear him his own son. By 1807 he had fathered an illegitimate son, so he knew it was possible. He was also interested in adopting his nephew Napoleon-Charles, the son of Louis Bonaparte and Hortense Beauharnais (who eventually became Napoleon III, but not by direct succession). Joseph, his older brother, always objected to this. Without a declared heir, the Bonaparte family knew they were powerful and influential, and that the succession issue was a risk to them all; but they could not agree on a solution amongst themselves. Until Napoleon remarried and produced a legitimate son, this difficult situation would continue.

Napoleon's use of his coronation to showcase his accumulation of power was dramatic, moving, spectacular – but not everyone was impressed. The Pope agreed to be present at the coronation (the date chosen was 21 December 1804) and even agreed that after the anointing, Napoleon would actually crown himself, taking the crown out of the Pope's hands. After the double-dealing and manipulation of the Concordat, the Pontiff must have despaired of Napoleon's excesses and just decided to go along with the flow. Additionally, the ultra-Royalists were angry that this 'hideous apostasy' of the coronation of an upstart foreigner meant that the Revolution they opposed was being legitimized and even sanctified. Josephine, of course, opposed it – officially she said it was too much about ambition and pride on Napoleon's part – but she knew too that it was held to celebrate the creation of a dynasty, and she had no child by Napoleon. Yet Napoleon still seemed committed to her: in fact they celebrated a religious wedding just before the coronation, making the most of the Pope's presence to supplement their earlier civil wedding, which in any case was never recognized by the Church.

Napoleon's family members fought like cat and dog throughout the arrangements, and at the actual event several were notable for their absence. Lucien and Jerome did not attend as Napoleon did not approve of their marriages, and they were not on speaking terms with him. His mother was visiting Lucien in Rome and therefore did not attend, but the artist David was instructed to paint her in the official painting of the coronation. Napoleon and his brother Joseph, who did attend, shared a quiet and proud moment thinking of their late father – if only Carlo could see them now! Joseph wanted to be heir, and as Napoleon's older brother was an obvious candidate, but his children were both girls so could also not solve the dynastic problem; as a result he was feeling hurt and rejected. Louis, married to Hortense, Josephine's daughter, although an invalid, would not accept being passed over in favour of his son.

Napoleon's sisters were also tiresome. All wanted to be called 'Highness', but all saw it as too demeaning to carry Josephine's train at the ceremony. Their attitude took much of the pleasure out of the coronation for the new Emperor.

But it would seem that several thousand soldiers were also against the elevation of Napoleon as Emperor, despite some vote-rigging and number-changing; and convinced Revolutionaries also saw the irony of what Napoleon was doing, still in the name of the Revolution. Parisian society mostly refused to be impressed by the lavish ceremony and remained suspicious of the Imperial project. Napoleon didn't trust them, preferring to listen to 'well-off peasants', and was concerned that the food supply and employment of the working class was more important: 'I fear insurrections caused by a shortage of bread – more than a battle against 200,000 men' (Markham, 1963: 135). A further marginalized segment of society who felt only opposition to Napoleon were well-connected women, many of whom had already been banished to the provinces or exiled from France altogether, such as Madame de Staël. Women were not to be allowed in the new Napoleonic 'Court' to avoid a 'petticoat influence', thought by Napoleon to have sapped the power of the Bourbon monarchy.

The people who were probably most impressed with the coronation were Napoleon's servants, including his old wet-nurse from Corsica, whom he invited to come and who enjoyed the rare privilege of an audience with the Pope. By this stage Napoleon seems to have been closer to his servants than anyone else, especially if they didn't complain or criticize. To increase personal support amongst his immediate associates, Napoleon created six imperial dignitaries, appointed in 1804, including a grand elector, arch-chancellor, arch-treasurer and other grand officers and new marshals of the Empire. These hand-picked supporters were happy with their new status, especially as grants of lands followed. To give them their due, around the altar of the coronation and around his new throne, Napoleon's court was to include not the foppish aristocrats of the past but men like him who had proved their worth in battle and service to the Republic.

Were foreigners impressed at the coronation? Those who saw Napoleon as an upstart, adventurer and parvenu were unlikely to change their minds as a result of a public relations exercise, and even though much of etiquette of the Bourbon monarchy was revived – the public ceremonial of the Imperial Court of Napoleon outshone the court of Louis XVI – it was widely seen as a front, a fake, an unconvincing attempt at pretend legitimacy. Napoleon realized that 'sovereigns must always be on show' and that 'kingship is an actor's part', but the foreign visitor to the Court saw Napoleon's exercise of power only, rather than the trappings of a traditional 'European Court'. It was all for a purpose: to imitate that which had the credibility Napoleon craved.

The demonstration of public support had important implications for other purposes. By 1804 Napoleon was actively planning the invasion of Britain, and amassed his army on the Normandy coast. They were preparing for the time the British navy would be defeated or distracted, allowing the invaders to cross the channel. The plebiscite and the coronation were intended to signal the army's enthusiasm for the venture, but in fact rather few soldiers voted at all, and of those who did, many opposed Napoleon's elevation. This would not have sent the right message to the British he was trying to intimidate, so Napoleon boosted the 'yes' military vote. Rigging the results in this way made no difference to the outcome, but it does expose Napoleon's anxiety about the mandate for his invasion plans.

The whole issue of election is one of Napoleon constantly seeking legitimacy, so it was indeed ironic that many of those not voting for him to be Life Consul and Emperor were in the army. Perhaps they knew something the civilians did not, or they had shed too much blood, sweat and tears to bring down the monarchy. When contemplating visiting ministers and princes coming to Paris from 'old Europe', Napoleon considered in his memoirs: 'would they be more ready to accept me, would they acknowledge the Revolution more willingly, if my head was girt with gold and diamonds and if God's representative had given me his blessing? Is this the price I have to pay to make them genuinely bend their knees, swallow their hatred and recognize that I, the son of the Revolution, am the equal of the greatest of the great?' (Cronin, 1971: 304).

Many observers have seen plebiscites as anti-democratic, used by dictators to gain approval then outlaw opposition. Plebiscites are conceded to be used by governments only when they are weak, to bolster themselves, as a form of manipulation by the management of an agenda. Napoleon's form of plebiscite offered people the choice to vote for him or not. This form of power has been popular in France, especially as since 1789 the idea of popular sovereignty was experienced, and this strategy avoided the formation of political parties. For this latter reason, it could also be used to confirm an autocratic power base, and was to be popular again in the rule of Napoleon III, to give an illusion of popular support.

Napoleon wanted to create a popular following as he wanted to create a new nobility to support him, based on the creation of a middle class whom he rewarded with land and honours – in 1802 he had created the *Legion d'Honneur*. Mostly military men, their numbers had increased to tens of thousands by 1814. It was in this class that he was to lay the strongest foundations of his popularity.

The importance of his popular election as Emperor cannot be separated from his growing obsession with dynastic succession. If he could create rules and procedures for succession, he could achieve legitimacy. Stability could also be established and civil war avoided if there were a clear set of rules to follow. It may be said that having dynastic procedures can be preferable to having a meritocracy, in order to achieve stability. Democratic and popular elections and plebiscites can pander to the lowest common denominator. Napoleon was caught in the middle here – he was not committed to a rule-based system of succession. He was adamant that he was best placed to personally select his successor. In a distorted meritocracy, the sole criterion here was the Emperor's selection of what constituted merit.

Napoleon's intense concern with who would succeed him was a function of his conviction that he alone was the heroic leader, he was the sole agent, and he was the main source of progress. From the point of view of most citizens, what the Emperor would do or say was just another factor in their daily battle for survival.

The coronation was about spectacle and popular legitimacy; combining a plebiscite with a popular spectacle, both designed to appeal to the masses. Napoleon was revelling in his extraordinary reputation at this point, and his ambitions were huge: he would soon lead his armies into spectacular victories, such as Austerlitz, Jena and Friedland. As his campaigns moved eastward, he was heralded by many as the liberator, the harbinger of a new approach to rule and to humanity. His coronation gave him a new lease of fame and respectability among his own people, justifying even more adventures.

Questions on leadership and power

How do you win hearts and inspire the mass of the people? To influence them to vote for you, and want to reward you, and to acknowledge you? Why should people follow you?

- Do you as a leader like shows of popular support and the adulation of the people working for you? Or does this not bother you?

(Continued)

(Continued)

- Is popular election used as a technique in your organization – either formally or informally? Is this a way to give a leader power and influence, and to justify certain leadership styles?

- How are leaders made in your organization, is there any system of voting involved, or any less formal way of gauging consensus?

- How have your projects and career been affected by this tradition?

- Is it important for a leader in your organization to be seen as a celebrity? Or can he or she be modest and humble and still be effective? What is your preferred approach?

- Do people in your organization like leaders who achieve major changes, especially those who raise its status? Or are leaders in consolidation mode also appreciated? Which is your approach as a leader?

- Why do people follow you as a leader? What is the role of inspiration and even demagogy?

INHERITANCE

Failure to create a dynasty, 1814: trying to gain the most elusive form of power — the kind that lasts

I am the French Revolution and I shall defend it.

Napoleon, 1804

Napoleon was obsessed by the problem of giving tradition and legitimacy to his throne and dynasty.

Markham, 1963, p133

Every prolongation of war, which does not allow the sovereigns to devote themselves seriously to stamping out the Jacobin ferment, which daily spreads, will soon threaten the existence of the thrones of Europe.

Austrian Emperor Francis I to Napoleon, April 1813

Napoleon had the defect of all parvenus, that of having too great an opinion of the class into which he had risen.

Stendhal, 1813

Your sovereigns born on the throne can let themselves be beaten 20 times and return to their capitals. I cannot do this because I am an upstart soldier. My domination will not survive the day when I cease to be strong and therefore feared.

Napoleon to Metternich, June 1813

A rumour spread in France – even among his marshals – that Napoleon was no longer fighting for France, but to satisfy his own personal pride.

Markham, 1963, pp202–203

Where today are the men one could employ for a bold measure? For ten years have they not been scattered, persecuted, extinguished – all the energetic men who rendered such great services at the decisive epoch of the Revolution?

Savary, the Minister of Police, to Cambaceres,
Chief Minister, December 1814

In 1814, with all that he had constructed crumbling around him, Napoleon's power base lacked what he wanted most: a guarantee of continuity beyond his own rule. Above all, he wanted a process of succession by inheritance. Napoleon had been elected hereditary Emperor and could nominate his successor, but in practice this was proving problematic. He had considered various options over the last decade. His young son was still an infant, and the Empress, Marie-Louise, was the daughter of the Austrian Emperor, a declared enemy now in a relatively effective coalition with Russia and Britain. By the spring of 1814 his military reversals had created an impasse and he faced abdication. The point here – the subject of this chapter, is the messy attempts at a transition of power at the end of Napoleon's regime, and the end of his hopes that his son would inherit. Nonetheless, the accession of Napoleon III in 1852 and the creation of the Second Empire was a posthumous achievement, a belated echo of adulation for *l'Empereur*.

From the day in May 1804 when Napoleon had been declared hereditary Emperor, the search for a successor began. Napoleon's family members increased their pressure on him to select one of them, creating damaging and embarrassing infighting, especially as their incompetence became apparent in military defeat and failure to accomplish any of the tasks Napoleon had given to them. By December 1809, Napoleon had started to approach the crowned heads of Europe for a potential spouse who could give him the son he craved. Caulaincourt, Napoleon's ambassador in Moscow, was sent to ask the Tsar for the hand of his younger sister; days later Josephine, who had been unable to conceive since her marriage to Napoleon, publicly declared her acceptance of a divorce. In February 1810, after an evasive answer from Russia, Napoleon approached the

Austrian Emperor with a view to marrying his daughter, the Archduchess Marie-Louise; they wed a month later by proxy in Vienna, to be solemnized on 1 April 1810 in France. In March 1811 their son, the King of Rome, was born amidst general rejoicing.

Throughout his marriage negotiations and his serious attempts to build a lasting dynasty, Napoleon was constantly at war, raising armies, concluding and breaking alliances, moving from one grand plan to another. In early 1808 he still had very grandiose ambitions – such as invading India with Tsar Alexander – but gathering doom pervaded many of his continental gains of earlier in the century. As Joseph's short reign as King of Spain came to an end and Napoleon had to recapture Madrid, the British became entrenched in Portugal and relations with Austria and the Tsar deteriorated, Napoleon considered his options. His disastrous invasion of Russia, with the loss of nearly half a million men, hundreds of thousands of horses and a huge amount of military hardware, may be seen as the beginning of the end. The Senate's promise to Napoleon of 350,000 new conscripts in January 1813 showed that he wasn't giving up, but the allies were closing in, especially when Austria declared war in August 1813.

As brother Joseph, appointed to defend Paris, was defeated, as enemy armies continued to increase in number, as Napoleon and his armies became exhausted after several days of forced marches and fighting in heavy rain, as he failed to follow-up half-won battles, as the Prussian general Blucher got away, and with losses in battle, sickness and desertion, the balance of numbers in the field weighed heavily against Napoleon. The huge losses he suffered at Leipzig as he waited too long for Marshal Ney sealed his defeat. Finally, Napoleon decided he wanted to die in battle, which he hoped might ensure the throne for his son, but he emerged unscathed, even after dozens of engagements. With a back-to-the-wall spirit he had managed what was left of the military machine of France single-handed for eight weeks, and he was exhausted.

With the defeat at Leipzig in October 1813, France lost Italy, northern Germany and Holland. Napoleon, still in denial of his defeat, refused to negotiate seriously, and would not accept the reduction of France to the borders of 1792. He then rapidly found himself cornered by the invading allies attacking him from all sides. But the Allies still hesitated to launch a full-scale invasion, even though the eastern frontiers of France were now wide open. They were still willing to negotiate with Napoleon – they were still afraid of him. France could keep her natural frontiers, marked by the Rhine, the Alps and the Pyrenees. The Legislature in France was getting involved, seeing a chance for peace, but Napoleon prorogued them, saying 'You are not the representatives of the nation. The true representative of the nation is myself. France has more need of me than I have need of France'. Castlereagh of Britain spoke for the other allies when he said 'Peace with Bonaparte, whatever the terms, will never be popular, because no one will believe that he can submit to his destiny' (Markham, 1963: 209).

Napoleon was now alone. For the previous 15 years he had insisted on passive obedience. The writer Stendhal (Markham, 1963: 210), in January 1814, wrote that 'the most vital people in Europe were, as a nation, nothing better than a corpse. That was what despotism did to one of the greatest geniuses who ever lived.' He could no longer raise conscripts, he faced a shortage of equipment, and increasing taxation inflamed public opinion whilst the treasury was constantly drained. His military campaign of January 1814 was regarded as brilliant, but Napoleon had no patience for defensive warfare. He was profoundly disappointed when he mistakenly expected Paris to hold out under the command of his brother Joseph, even though his armies in the capital were outnumbered more than four to one: 50,000 to more than 220,000.

It was only when the Austrians and Prussians finally marched on Paris that Napoleon started to consider peace on any terms. The Bourbon Standard was raised at Bordeaux, and the National Guard was asking him for peace. The legislative body was urging Napoleon to accept the peace treaties, and he retorted by reminding them that four million Frenchmen had voted for him. 'I want no tribunes of the people: let them not forget that I am the great tribune', but these were empty words: Napoleon's forces were too depleted. Then Napoleon's conniving double-agent foreign minister Talleyrand revealed to the allies Napoleon's weak political hold on Paris, and they had captured a letter from Napoleon to Marie-Louise in which he had rashly revealed his plans. The arrival of the allies at the undefended city gates caught Napoleon unawares. The Parisians, meanwhile, had evacuated with their valuables, and buried their money in their gardens.

Napoleon then made a last-ditch attempt to ensure that the Empress and the King of Rome could assume power in his place. He encouraged them to go to Rambouillet on the Loire to escape the occupation of Paris, and wanted the Senate, the Council of State and remaining troops to all gather there, especially to prevent his wife and son being sent back to Austria. Joseph and Talleyrand sent the Empress and the infant King of Rome to Rambouillet as instructed. Their carriage was attacked by Cossacks, so they had to walk the last three miles on foot, but they went alone. Contrary to Napoleon's plans, Talleyrand and the Government stayed in Paris. On 30 March 1814 Paris capitulated, to Napoleon's old enemy Tsar Alexander. Talleyrand made a token attempt to go to the city gates as if to leave, but without his passport the authorities there wouldn't let him go – that was his excuse for staying to serve the invaders. The chances of establishing a Regency and therefore a form of Napoleonic dynasty were greatly diminished without the Empress, and meanwhile the government led by Talleyrand was left in Paris to negotiate with the enemy. Marie-Louise realized it was a mistake to have left the capital, but had accepted the move for herself and her son as it was in Napoleon's letter to Joseph, but she was never intended to leave Paris without the government.

There was no big support for the Bourbons in Paris and the allies (entering Paris as liberators of the French from Napoleon, not as occupiers) were not convinced of the wisdom of restoring them. But when their armies entered Paris with white arm-bands (designed only to identify the Allied troops and distinguish them from the French), it looked as if they had declared for the white flag of the Bourbons. Talleyrand, rapidly forming a provisional government, persuaded the Senate to proclaim the deposition of Napoleon. The throne could still have been saved for the King of Rome, and the possibility of a Regency under the Empress was not excluded by the Allies; but the army told Napoleon that they would not march. They had had too much of war and wanted peace, and many of the officers had become wealthy under the Empire and did not want their fine Parisian houses to be torched. At this shocking defiance, Napoleon wrote out his conditional abdication in favour of his son, and started burning all the papers in his study. But as more generals defected, including the previously-loyal Marmont who went over to the Austrians with 12,000 men, on 6 April 1814 Napoleon was forced into unconditional abdication, mostly by his own marshals, persuaded by Talleyrand: 'Everyone has betrayed me.'

The Tsar, who was staying in Talleyrand's house, had considered three options: he could make peace with Napoleon; he could set up Marie-Louise as a Regent for the Napoleonic dynasty for her son; or he could restore the Bourbons. This was the moment Talleyrand had been waiting for. It must be the Bourbons. A Regency would only work if Napoleon had fallen in battle, otherwise he would still be in control. Napoleon had to go otherwise there would just be more war. The Tsar signed the declaration to appoint a provisional government, convened the Senate, announced that Napoleon was deposed, and invited Louis XVIII to reclaim his throne.

So, on 6 April 1814, Napoleon was forced to abdicate without success-fully concluding an established line of succession. The confirmation of his removal was shown by the Bourbon restoration, his banishment to the island of Elba and the permanent removal of the Empress Marie-Louise and the King of Rome away from Paris and then to Austria. He faced overwhelming military defeat, was rejected by his father-in-law the Austrian Emperor, and his family and other supporters deserted him. The will to fight had gone out of his soldiers and his people after a decade of heavy-handed, despotic rule. One of the greatest disappoint-ments, comparatively unexpected and of deep regret, was the failure of the Parisians to defend their city, and the rapidity with which they wel-comed the return of the Bourbons.

On what was to be his first abdication in April 1814, Napoleon was allowed by the allies to rule the sovereign principality of Elba, and could even keep his Emperor title. Meanwhile the King of Rome, taken to Vienna and brought up as the Duke of Reichstadt, was accepted by loyal Bonapartists as Napoleon II from 1821 (when Napoleon died) until his own death in 1832, although apparently he never used his father's title. He was eventually succeeded as Emperor of the French by Napoleon's nephew, the son of his brother Louis and step-daughter Hortense Beauharnais, Josephine's daughter. This was Charles Louis Napoleon Bonaparte (1808–73), who became Napoleon III, Emperor of the French from 1852–70, the leader of the Second (and last) Empire.

The story of Napoleon's second abdication, to St Helena, in 1815 after the battle of Waterloo, is well known. Even though his hundred days' comeback was very nearly successful, he did not achieve the final form of power he coveted: to have established a new dynasty amongst the royal houses of Europe. His pact with power failed him in the end.

Reflections on leadership and power

- Napoleon wanted to leave behind a dynasty, with princes bearing his name, officially to sustain the achievements of the Revolution, but unofficially for more personal reasons.

- He would give up his power and position if he knew that his wife and son would carry on his line and gain legitimacy and respect, and succeed him as Emperor – dynastic power was his greatest goal, but it always eluded him, despite his efforts to gain it.

- Napoleon was always disappointed that he could never be seen as an equal with the established monarchs of Europe.

- He allowed this to overshadow many of his less well-known achievements in reforming the law, society and administration generally.

- The creation of the Second Empire of the 1850s and 1860s was a result of Napoleon's efforts and legacy, but perhaps not in the way he envisaged.

- In spite of everything, the nostalgic appeal of the cult of Bonapartism continues, and the Napoleonic romance of greatness would still seem to survive.

Even when faced with evidence to the contrary, Napoleon was coming to regard himself as invincible and convinced that he could hold onto the power and status he enjoyed as Emperor and continue to play his enemies off against each other. He could keep winning battles – he was the great Napoleon, feared by the crowned heads of Europe. He had produced a son, who in the course of time might succeed him.

The crucial moment, when Napoleon realized that his almost endless series of military victories had come to an end and efforts to create a dynasty were over, was to occur in 1814. Napoleon had been decisively beaten in battle and was forced to abdicate; he could live with this, if his beloved son (still a baby) had succeeded in his place, under the Regency of his wife. But the young King of Rome and Marie-Louise had been forced to flee, with no opportunity to inherit. The immediate cry of the Parisians for the Bourbon restoration, without thought of continuing with Napoleon or his successors, meant that he was revealed as just General Bonaparte, the adventurer, the parvenu – no different than he was in 1799, no more legitimate, and no more likely to lead a new dynasty. This painful realization of how naïve he had been and the lack of loyal support among even his family members, fellow military men and his ministers in the government, must have been more traumatic than the battlefield defeats.

Why did the Parisians give up so easily? The answer might be found in the writings of Machiavelli, who suggests that people benefiting from an old order will hang on to it and resist change more fiercely than those recently coming to a new order will defend theirs. So the aristocrats thriving on Bourbon rule were more enthusiastic to revive their fortunes than the members of the nouveau riche of Napoleon's time were committed to protecting the new order. As Machiavelli had theorized, and as he described in *The Prince*, Napoleon's regime was 'unfamiliar, and his supporters were not certain that he would live up to his promises'. Napoleon could 'not satisfy all so he must have the means to force his supporters to keep supporting him even when they have second thoughts otherwise he will lose power' – and this is what happened (Machiavelli, The Prince).

In fact the fragility of Napoleonic rule had been evident for some time. He had been shocked and incensed when, during an attempted military coup of 1812, it was announced that he had been killed in Russia, none of his ministers thought of proclaiming his son, the infant King of Rome, as Napoleon II.

One of the reasons for his mistaken confidence in his subordinates' loyalty and his diminishing grasp of reality might have been the lack of feedback he received and the absence of a free press. He had argued, 'if the press is not bridled, I shall not remain three days in power' (Markham, 1963: 100). So he clearly knew that his grasp on power was tenuous.

It could have all been very different. With the constitution of the Life Consulate, Napoleon had been able to develop a power base more abso-lute than any Bourbon monarch, especially because the institutions of the *ancien régime*, which might have moderated his power, had been swept away by the Revolution. But it was still not assumed to be legiti-mate in the way he coveted.

Napoleon's efforts to build a dynastic power base and ensure the inheri-tance of his son were doomed to failure, especially after 1812, for three specific reasons. First, he faced more and more military failures which undermined his credibility. Second, his father-in-law the Austrian Emperor never really recognized him as 'family' despite Napoleon's marriage to his daughter, and the idea of a joint Bonaparte–Habsburg dynasty was short-lived, especially as Napoleon continued to pursue more and more territorial conquests at odds with his in-laws and their allies. Third, Napoleon's own family members were greedy and opportu-nistic, and in any case unimpressive as potential future leaders.

Military defeats, given that his Empire rested on military success, inevi-tably undermined Napoleon's chance of establishing a lasting dynasty. The invasion of Russia in June 1812 was an act of spectacular hubris, launched on the assumption that under threat of invasion the Tsar would join forces with Napoleon, his fellow Emperor. Though victorious at Borodino, Napoleon never completely redeemed his reputation from the costly retreat from Moscow, and the whole country felt the loss of half a million men and horses. It ultimately led to the war of the fourth coali-tion and his military defeat at Leipzig. He had hoped to stitch together a new modernizing order from a patchwork of old monarchies; but his power was ultimately based on military conquests and the threat of constant economic and social chaos he could engender among his enemies (as an autocrat himself, he never saw or desired the potential for an international revolutionary movement). If this threat was reduced due to military failure, Napoleon was much less dangerous. He could survive only by constant war, and this meant that his enemies had to remove him from power; the big question was whether he could be trusted as an exiled emperor – whilst he lived he would always be a possible source of discontent and rebellion in their lands.

Amazingly, Napoleon could still keep going after the retreat from Moscow. The Russians had also suffered enormously in 1812. Austria still feared Napoleon but liked Russia less, and Metternich, the foreign minister, did not want to see what he called the 'total destruction of Bonaparte' whilst he was useful as a buffer against Russia. The fourth coalition was strong, but by his skill in diplomacy, making the occasional concessions and exploiting the war-weariness of Europe, Napoleon could keep going. He also made the most of the fear of many of Europe's sovereigns of the outbreak of popular movements like the French Revolution, and their jealousy over who owned which territories. So Napoleon could ensure continuity for his regime for some time.

In particular, Napoleon could have survived if his ambitions were confined within France's natural frontiers. But, as Emperor, he felt obliged to keep pursuing the Grand Empire expansion plan. He was not ready to face the loss of prestige involved in the sacrifice of the Empire, and realized that this would mean the end of his autocracy. Napoleon therefore rejected the first wave of peace overtures in June 1813 at Dresden. Metternich, the foreign minister of the Austrian Emperor, pointed out to him: 'If your Majesty loses this opportunity for peace, what limit can there be to revolutions for us?' Everyone was tired of war, and it was seen that any efforts at peace depended on Napoleon's next moves – most of the time he was rejecting them. He was still amassing armies, recruiting more conscripts and boasting that he could probably put together six or seven hundred thousand men, but he was suffering a shortage of horses, having lost 80,000 in Russia. Wellington, writing from the south of France in November 1813 confirmed that 'all except the officials are sick of Bonaparte, because there is no prospect of peace with him' (Markham, 1963: 210).

So it became imperative that Napoleon be beaten in the field. As we have heard, it was observed that one should 'expect a defeat whenever the Emperor attacks in person. So attack and defeat his lieutenants whenever you can. Once they are beaten, assemble all your forces against

Napoleon and give him no respite' (Markham, 1963: 206). By early
1814, ministers and generals were defecting: there was no constitutional
way for them to contradict Napoleon in government, so Napoleon's
first route to established power – through military conquest – was thus
unsustainable in the long term.

The second route to legitimizing his succession was through his strategic
marriage alliance. He had married the Austrian Archduchess Marie-
Louise, the daughter of the Emperor Francis I, and their son was born
in March 1811. Francis would have considered a Bonaparte-Habsburg
dynasty in France, but could not trust Napoleon to stop war-mongering.
Napoleon meanwhile complained of hostility from Austria, but Francis
was bound to refuse to help France keep the Confederation of the Rhine,
and wanted France to give up the Grand Duchy of Warsaw. On 26 June
1813, Napoleon had a nine-hour meeting with Metternich, Francis' chief
minister, but couldn't accept his demands for an evacuation from French
territories in Europe, and began to realize that Francis was just not supporting him. Metternich called Napoleon's treaties only truces, warning
him that 'today you can still conclude peace; tomorrow it may be too
late' (Markham, 1963: 205).

Napoleon's derisory offers of peace to Austria had been made because
he didn't think Francis would fight his son-in-law, especially as he had
given Marie-Louise the title of Regent while he was away from France.
But Napoleon was being naïve, and the bonds of family were just not the
same for northern Europeans. Meanwhile if Francis could make peace
with Russia, Napoleon was no longer useful to him. The fact that he was
a son-in-law was immaterial to the pragmatic Austrian, who had none
of the cultural obligations to family members felt by Napoleon. So the
young King of Rome (as he was called by Napoleon), Francis' grandson,
was never allowed to return to France after he and his mother fled in
1814.

Third, the Bonaparte family also undermined Napoleon's efforts to cre-
ate a dynasty. They had all received many titles and honours, all out of
Napoleon's sense of family obligation, and were part of his efforts to
create a new European dynasty. He had made Joseph King of Naples,
Lucien Prince of Canino, Louis was King of Holland, Jerome became
King of Westphalia, and his two sisters married Napoleon's generals –
Leclerc and Murat. But none of them were convincing as successors,
and none really supported him in his hour of need. Napoleon's brothers
were a disaster. Jerome gave up Westphalia without a fight, then bought
a splendid chateau; Louis lost his kingdom of Holland and wrote com-
plaining letters to Francis, who then published them for all to see. Joseph

was unable to conquer, rule or defend any of his domains, and meanwhile was in league with Napoleon's old friend and rival Bernadotte, who had defected to Sweden.

In the end few people shared Napoleon's insistent conviction that he was above all fighting for France: it was seen that maintaining his grip on power had become an end in itself. As with so many leaders, power became a personal goal, irrelevant to others and contradictory to other strategic objectives, and eventually undermining authority due to perceived selfishness and self-serving activities. Securing the succession is not necessarily the most important measure of leadership success, and was not exactly the oath to which Napoleon swore at his coronation. Being an illegitimate leader and having to compensate for this with genuine achievements such as improvements to the well-being of the followers might not be such a poor objective. When legitimacy is mostly a perception of the presence or lack of personal status, it can look like vanity.

Yet there is no escaping the romance of Napoleon's story and his epic rise and fall, which captured the imagination of generations. The presence at the time of brilliant writers, in France and elsewhere – such as Stendhal, Chateaubriand and Tolstoy – built up the legend which has continued, and his fame over the centuries has been ensured.

Whatever the efforts of an individual leader, the reality of the legacy further down the track will be seen in the attitude of the next generation. Legends are changed and embellished or destroyed as they are handed down. Napoleon's legacy might not have been quite what he intended, but there is no doubt that a legacy exists. It would be a rare discussion of leaders in history where Napoleon's name was not mentioned, though perhaps not in the context which he would have wanted.

Although Napoleon failed in his quest to see his son succeed him as Emperor, the Napoleonic cachet has never entirely died, and enabled his nephew, Charles Louis Napoleon, to come to power and create the Second Empire in the later-nineteenth century. Napoleon so wanted to leave behind a dynasty, a new line of princes bearing his name who would sustain the achievements of the Revolution – whatever that meant to him. He was prepared to give up his power and position if he knew that his wife and son would carry on his line and gain legitimacy and respect. Legitimate power was his greatest goal, which always eluded him. Although the first empire of the late eighteenth and early nineteenth centuries was followed by the second empire of the 1850s and 1860s, and although the nostalgic appeal of the cult of Bonapartism continues, he was always disappointed that he could never be an equal with the crowned heads of Europe. This failure overshadowed many of his other achievements in creating the *Code Napoleon*, new constitutions, his reform of the law, society and administration generally.

One of the reasons for this was that Napoleon's legitimacy was based on military power. The country needed peace, but he could not provide it. He argued that 'peace is the foremost of needs, as it is the foremost of glories' in 1802, but he knew that when he was no longer successful militarily, when he lost his ability to reward others, he would have lost everything. He insisted that 'the crowned heads understand nothing: I am not afraid of old Europe (Gallo, 1997a: 249), in 1805, but by 1814 he was fighting desperately for his throne.

Why was Napoleon so keen on creating a dynasty? He had been part of the Revolution that had broken down the old traditions of inheritance, of those born into power and privilege, property and wealth, with access to education, people born to power. Napoleon wanted to create a new kind of inheritance, one he had had to fight for, and having struggled so much he wanted to have what others took for granted.

The problem of succession was the main issue here, and for Europe at this time this was a new problem – most of Europe was run by established dynasties. The Revolution had attempted to create legitimate decision-making administrative bodies that drew on meritocracy and popular representation through political parties. Napoleon undermined these efforts, concentrating power in himself and generating new administrative initiatives personally, such as the *Code Napoleon* and the Concordat. There was no mode of succession here, except inheritance, which he could pass on. Dynastic succession by inheritance was built in to his being elected emperor, as it was widely believed that it was hard to trust others except family members and offspring.

Owners of a family business frequently want to pass it on to the next generation – this is a large part of the legacy and inheritance they can give. It is hard to resist the parental desire to favour one's children, and there is a widespread belief that the recipients of an inheritance should be the children, and that 'inheritance legitimizes the exercise of power'.

Throughout Napoleon's career, inheritance was a significant argument to justify many of his decisions. His parents Carlo and Letizia had to establish their aristocratic antecedents to enable Joseph and Napoleon to be eligible for patronage, to go to school in France and gain French nationality. Their Corsican heritage was a problem and their children were bullied for it, but when they became French they could join the new middle class of post-Revolution nobility, especially through military achievement. Napoleon also used the concept of providing for future inheritance as part of his system of patronage, giving vast tracts of land to his supporters to create something like a landed aristocracy in order for them to pass on their wealth. This was a major preoccupation of many in previous centuries: one of the most important tasks of all was to pass on whatever they had created to the next generation. It may be only in recent times, in only some parts of the world, that this is no longer so significant.

Questions on leadership and power

What will be your legacy? What will you leave behind you when you have gone? What will others inherit from you and what control might you have over this?

- Is the process of succession to your business, achievements, things you value clear to you? Or will you leave everything to chance?

- What ideally might be the legacy you would like to leave behind you? Is this realistic, and will successors carry on your policies and strategies to another generation?

- Or has your aim for a legacy to leave behind you always eluded you, despite your efforts to gain it?

- Do you feel you have achieved the status for which you have been looking, and see yourself as an equal with those you admire?

- Are you remembered for the things you thought most important? Or maybe something else? Do the people carrying on your work see it in the way that you do?

- What might others inherit from you, and will they respect it as you have?

EXECUTIVE REFLECTIONS ON LEADERSHIP AND POWER

Comments by readers asked about the eight manifestations of power and how they have used these or been affected by these in their careers

1. PATRONAGE

As an expatriate running a factory in China I was the 'patron' for many of my local staff, and even when they wanted to leave the company I still helped them – especially because after they left us they soon realized that 'the grass wasn't greener' and came back to our company.

Patronage is very big in China, everyone has their higher-level supporters who look after them, they always surround themselves with people they know and trust, and there's little criticism of those in power by their followers. As a result, in China when there is a change of leadership, everyone is worried and nothing happens until there is a reshuffling. By contrast, in the Netherlands, this practice is uncommon.
Manager of manufacturing plant from the Netherlands

I had a 'patron' to join the Royal Navy in so far that my father was a naval officer and encouraged me, and when I joined up, more senior officers took me under their wing. Now I'm captain of a large yacht I'm a sort of 'patron' of my younger crew members, supporting them to gain promotion. They know I'm trying to help them and are very willing and loyal as a result. *Former Royal Navy officer*

I tried to be 'patron' for a young chap so that he could learn my business and then become my partner and help me out, as I was too busy to do it all by myself. But never again, as he stole my customers and set up in competition against me. *Technical surveyor, Shipping Industry*

I worked for a well-known and very rich family in the USA. The second generation, although benefiting from the patronage of the first generation, were too much in their shadow, and lost touch with the realities of the business. *Interior designer, New York*

I work for a family-owned business, founded by the father, and the son lives in his shadow – but he just doesn't have the personality for the opportunities his father wants to give him. Yet his father, acting as his 'patron' as it were, wants to keep giving him more and more chances in the company. Sometimes, the father will disrupt the work of ten people to give his son a task, and he's useless at it so it just wastes everyone's time. *Administrator in defence industry, UK*

A student of mine was conducting research on the hiring practices of leading accounting firms and discovered that the majority went to the same few universities. This gave them an instant network and the older and more experienced ones could be patrons of the younger ones, a bit like the practice of mentoring that they already had at their university. To a certain extent it happens on a national scale, in politics, and has attracted criticism for being a 'closed shop' and evidence of cronyism. *University professor*

Some professionals in niche professions deliberately try to reserve the top places for themselves and the younger people they like to whom they bestow 'patronage' and keep out anyone else from joining their 'club'. They create ridiculous barriers to entry and find fault with anyone on ridiculous grounds who wants to join their 'club' but whom they don't like or don't think is good enough. They also want to keep out anyone who apparently threatens their position. Some of these professionals are lazy and don't move with the times, so their system of 'patronage' keeps out new ideas and new techniques which they haven't bothered to learn, and they try to discredit them to preserve their own dominance in their professions. So they become less and less competitive and more and more behind the times, and the young people they 'patronize' perpetuate the system and don't rock the boat, because they are in the 'club'. *Former young banker, now in consulting, from South America*

I live in a small country where politics are sharply divided between two political parties. Many people work as volunteers for one or the other parties. When one party is kicked out of power and another comes in, the successful party wants to reward its loyal followers. So they are given jobs in the public sector. Some of them are completely incompetent in these jobs, and they are replacing someone who was quite good and who had several years of experience (depending on how long the previous party was in power). But the people want these positions and the party wants to reward them. I guess this is a form of patronage. *Retired expatriate*

2. MERIT

I always relied on my own skill-set, my ability and hard work and application to progress my career and develop my expertise as a manager and a consultant. But I came to realize that ability is not enough, and is less highly regarded depending on the type of organization where a person is employed. Intellectual and specialist ability is less rewarded in the government sector, for instance. *Consultant, originally from the USA, working in the Middle East*

I have always tried to succeed on the basis of my individual knowledge and expertise because I don't do fear and manipulation as leadership techniques. I'm a straightforward technical guy who has been promoted for running projects and units and delivering results and saving money for my company by putting businesses back on their feet, just that. *Manager of manufacturing plant from the Netherlands*

Merit has opened many doors in my career and company. The main advantage is that it works as an introduction card. But this kind of 'publicity' is very slow, and it is not good as a marketing strategy. So merit is good to start with. *Team leader, private sector business, South America*

It seems to me that even if you are very good at your job, that won't help you if your bosses want to get rid of you for some reason. Having huge ability and being an over-achiever can be seen as threatening.

Many people who are like this are also naïve and don't realize that they are on the list of people not having their contracts renewed. Maybe they are too busy doing their work! *Management consultant and trainer*

I have always tried to do things for the long-term strategic good of the business, and not for personal gain, but have faced severe criticism by those who don't see it this way and are convinced I'm doing it for personal motives – but they can't work out what these motives are! *Consultant, originally from the USA, working in the Middle East*

I think it's nice to be good at what you do and of course, if you are a perfectionist you want to be as good as you possibly can be, but I've come to realize that it's much more effective to be a sycophant and be liked by the most important people who will then help you. *Former young banker, now in consulting, from South America*

3. CHARISMA

I have met very few charismatic people in my life, but when I do meet one, there is a huge 'wow' factor. This person walks into the room and everyone notices and is somehow awed and stops talking and looks. It's indefinable but electric. *University professor*

Charisma is a tool that works fine in our teams. It motivates everybody and ensures the communication of goals and strategies. But when the context in which we're operating becomes tough, it is not sufficient to maintain self-motivation in all the different kinds of team members. For some of those, another kind of motivation must be applied. Charisma is definitely a 'better to have' skill but is not enough for an all-round leader in all situations. *Team leader, private sector business, South America*

I've had many bosses who were good at passing off as their own work the efforts of others, especially when they were charismatic and came over as convincing to others. *Former Royal Navy officer*

I had a very charming and charismatic research assistant who was very pleasant to have around and everyone liked her, but she didn't really use her charisma for a higher purpose, just to get other people to do her work for her. She was always being offered high-powered and well-paid jobs but was not ambitious, so in a way she wasted this 'gift'. *Management consultant and trainer*

I wouldn't say I was charismatic but I do have referent power, at least people seem to like to work with me because I'm 'nice' or at best reasonable and fair, which I think goes a long way. *Manager of manufacturing plant from the Netherlands*

I don't rate the importance of charisma on its own, unless it's backed by an ability to make sound, evidence-based logical arguments. I'm not drawn to charismatic leaders because they are likeable or inspirational – but this ability needs to be combined with tough decision making to be influential to me personally. *Consultant, originally from the USA, working in the Middle East*

4. COUP D'ETAT

I have always 'seized power' by taking opportunities whenever they came up, and put my hand up to manage the company's subsidiary in China, at a time when most other people in the company didn't want to go, and thought it was impossible to do much, as it was too difficult. But I never give up on difficult tasks, and did well volunteering for difficult assignments. *Manager of manufacturing plant from the Netherlands*

I always seized opportunities when I could but I did them because I thought I could make a useful contribution to the business or organization, but others questioned my motives and wondered why I was doing it and were very suspicious. I can quite see why some people never volunteer for anything. *Consultant, originally from the USA, working in the Middle East*

My background is as a project manager, so I must suddenly take responsibility when I get the chance. When 'seizing' an opportunity you need to respond to the needs of the stakeholders, and offer them a sense of security (or the idea that someone is taking care of reducing their risks), and the creation of a leader for all the team members. I think that the only disadvantage in taking opportunities when you can is the high levels of stress that the person assumes for him/herself. *Team leader, private sector business, South America*

Seizing power the way that Napoleon did it is not just taking advantage of opportunities as they come up, it's more like staging a boardroom coup, or leading a takeover bid by one company of another. Many of the most famous corporate leaders have done it, or had it done to them. It also can happen to politicians, when the members of the inner sanctum gang-up and force someone out, then push their favoured candidate in. There is often a feeling of mutiny about it, and the person on the receiving end feels abandoned, cheated, let-down and booted-out. *University professor*

5. MANIPULATION

You can survive in a manipulative business culture if you don't leave yourself exposed to others' influences and if you retain a superficially sound and amicable working relationship with others. But astute colleagues will notice the signs and withdraw their trust from you, and you may gain the reputation for not being a good team-player. Some colleagues may withhold information from you (especially for their benefit) which might make it difficult for you to do your job. *Consultant, originally from the USA, working in the Middle East*

I have used 'accomplishment bonuses' in order to motivate good performance from our team members. It had good results, but I recognize that it implies some risks like promoting selfishness instead of team work or leadership. So it's manipulating behaviour, basically. *Team Leader, private sector business, South America*

Others were promoted ahead of me as I didn't have the ability to play politics as much as they did. I was too busy doing my job, and other people's jobs. I didn't know how to play the game, and if I did know I didn't want to. I was always too much of a team-player, and too transparent, not willing to compromise – too honest, basically. *Former Royal Navy officer*

There are organizational cultures where manipulation is not seen in a negative way – it is a way of avoiding confrontation with others, it can include withholding negative or difficult news, and it can mean pleasing others. But it's not healthy in a competitive business environment and can damage the business in the long term if there is no real substance. *Consultant, originally from the USA, working in the Middle East*

I applied for an internal position in my company but one of the senior managers to whom I would have reported just didn't want me to get the job. So he said that if I applied for the job I would have to move to another country, which was much more expensive and meant paying a much higher rate of tax. But the pay was the same. So it was a no-brainer and I was forced to withdraw. *Management consultant and trainer*

I was trying to get citizenship of a country where I had worked for many years and I scrupulously followed all the requirements, including attending courses and filling out every kind of form imaginable, and attending the office for applicants every week, sometimes twice a week. After nearly a year I was finally given the documents. My friends said I should have got to know the right people, paid bribes etc. etc. but I just couldn't do this. *Orchestral musician*

Developing your power and influence through your reputation for intellectual application only works in less political environments. In some organizations other factors are equally important or more so. Political allegiances, manipulation, interpersonal relationships, the deliberate withholding of information and a focus on pleasing people – these activities can be much more important than the provision of evidence-based assessment of an issue. *Consultant, originally from the USA, working in the Middle East*

Being more interested in manipulation and political intrigue means you lose the common touch. If you are not in contact with the fairly ordinary people at the sharp end of your business you run the risk of being out of touch with what really matters. *Interior designer, New York*

There can be an increasing level of manipulation as a person rises in an organization and is forced to become part of the intrigue, and I for one become more uncertain and more uncomfortable when this happens. I don't have a secret agenda for myself but I find myself working hard behind the scenes to find out the secret agendas of others so I can find out what's going on and why. *Consultant, originally from the USA, working in the Middle East*

As I travel around the world, I notice that politicking seems to be a feature of people from the 'old world' rather than the 'new world'. For example, I went to work in a branch of a UK company in New Zealand. The culture of this branch was completely different from branches where I've worked in the UK. The teamwork was much stronger in New Zealand, perhaps due to people playing sports much more. Playing politics in the office was definitely not tolerated. *Insurance company manager, New Zealand*

The leader of a group of enthusiast/hobbyists of which I'm a member is very competent and helpful, and is very generous with his time, and really manages much of the administration of the group. But he only likes and will help people who agree with him. I bought some supplies for the group, but he found an article that said these supplies were not useful, and then criticized me and anyone else who bought these supplies, enjoying crowing over people he regarded as wrong. To keep him happy most people are quite subservient to him as they don't want to do the work, but he is laughed at and not respected for his bossy manner. *Member of hobby group*

I really dislike this kind of power and if I find any of my staff in China doing deals behind my back I would sack them on the spot. My sales guys were sometimes doing deals with purchasing managers of clients, and my purchasing manager was also making private arrangements with external sales people, and I just won't tolerate it. The Dutch way is to be very straight, and although I'm willing to make cultural adaptations, this is non-negotiable. *Manager of manufacturing plant from the Netherlands*

Developing your emotional and cognitive intelligence is an important step in determining when and where to apply your 'cleverness' for its best impact. I have found that applying your diplomatic skills and trying to read the demeanour and motives of others can help with delivering a message to get results. It's all about surviving in a manipulative environment, even if you are trying not to be manipulative yourself – but you do end up being a bit like those around you. *Consultant, originally from the USA, working in the Middle East*

When you are far away from HQ – as when I was in China – it's important to have someone back in HQ who can tell you what is really happening and can support your interests when you are not there. I had a problem with politicking behind my back at HQ and the only way I could deal with this was to go above the head of my immediate boss and try to find out the real story. *Manager of manufacturing plant from Netherlands*

6. FEAR

I had a boss who was going through my performance appraisal with me and was picking on one tiny piece of negative feedback I'd got and ignoring all the efforts I had made beyond the call of duty. I tried to defend myself and he threatened me with a C grade when I'd had a B+ before. So I was forced to accept a B grade, when I was definitely not worse than I had been before. I later found out that he'd been told by the Chairman to not increase anyone's performance scores as the company had no money to give pay rises. I was intimidated to accept something I thought wasn't fair. *Management consultant and trainer*

I worked in an office where the manager ruled through fear – the fear of losing your job, when you had a mortgage and children at expensive schools. As a result the people being terrorized didn't do their best work, they think negatively about the concept of loyalty and really want to leave, but dare not, until they can get another job. Personally, this pushed me into setting up my own business. *Interior designer, New York*

The use of intimidation as a resource to achieve goals is just a type of management style that should be used only in special cases. Usually my team is composed of very proactive and dynamic people. This kind of team member needs a less coercive approach, and a more 'coaching and promoting' style of management from his or her leader. I think that the use of intimidation is not good, because it doesn't create a sense of belonging in the teams, and it erodes the relationships between team members, so it has to be used carefully. *Team leader, private sector business, South America*

Intimidation is used extensively by leaders to push their agendas. This leadership style is rewarded where status and the 'chain of command' is the leadership style of choice. I have used it in the past when others have tried to use it on me. It's not effective unless you can back it up with substance and outcomes. Perhaps it's best used in moderation and combined with merit-based authority. The advantage for a leader is that it will make things happen quickly, and you can leave your personal mark. The disadvantages are that you can cause alienation; resentment in others leading to low morale; lack of initiative; and no feedback from others when things are going wrong. *Consultant, originally from the USA, working in the Middle East*

7. ELECTION

We have a works council at our organization, and regularly people working there stand for election. If the employees like someone and respect them, they will vote for them. If they don't, they get almost no votes at all. It's very personal and subjective, and almost has nothing to do with the role or tasks expected of them as office-holders if they are elected. *Management consultant and trainer*

The chairman of a network of volunteer groups who was elected by the members enjoys the position of power this gives him. An ex-banker, he likes wearing a suit, having his picture taken shaking hands with people who have won awards, writing the welcome section in the newsletter, and generally being a figurehead. He's fairly harmless as he lets the groups get on with whatever they like, but he is a bit of a 'stuffed shirt' and could do more to help, so he's a bit of a joke. *Member of hobby group*

When I have been elected to positions of power in the past, it's a lottery as to what works and how you might get in. I've appealed to the common good showing how most people could benefit from my leadership. The use of strong rhetoric and some emotion and compelling arguments has worked. When you have the support of the majority, at least in the short term, you can achieve some quick wins, because you have the legitimacy of your position. But once a difficult decision is needed the collateral goodwill dissipates very soon, all the others think that decisions will be made by election, and you can alienate a power base quite quickly if you aren't willing to compromise. *Consultant, originally from the USA, working in the Middle East*

I stood for election to a chamber of commerce position but I didn't get voted in. I think it was because I was the only one who was a consultant (and a woman) and the others were captains of industry. They were going to use the chamber as a chaps' drinking club and could swap yarns about their problems and successes. They were afraid I would keep trying to sell them consulting services and probably that I would keep pushing the chamber to organize prestigious events (also to sell more consulting). I actually just wanted to be part of the community as we were all expatriates, but they were looking for other motives in me which weren't there, and they didn't trust me because I wasn't one of them. *Management consultant*

As Napoleon said when seeking election as Emperor, 'men need simple words, strong and clear ideas, and dazzling ceremonies'. As Lenin said, coming to power in war-torn Russia, 'peace, bread, land'. Churchill is famous for his 'blood, sweat and tears' speech. Simplicity in an elector message to try to drum up popular support would seem to be a basic requirement. *University lecturer*

8. INHERITANCE

I had a client who was the descendant of a very wealthy family. You got the feeling that when you were with him, every minute of his time was worth about half a million bucks. But he was good at hiring people who were capable and letting them get on with it. The trouble was that he inherited a business on the downhill slide. His forebears had been feudal. He inherited huge union/labour relations problems which his ancestors had ignored. *Interior designer, New York*

My boss, the founder of a family-owned business, keeps wanting his son to take over from him, or at least play a key role in the company, but the younger man lacks the confidence, is full of doubt of his abilities, and every project he tackles just fizzles out. The hierarchy is very flat, the leadership is laissez-faire style, and everyone is very polite and indirect. So, as the son doesn't get much feedback, he doesn't get much better at his job, so this 'dynasty' is unlikely to carry on for the long term. *Administrator in defence industry, UK*

I worked for a company chairman who was the grandson of the founder. It was no fun for him trying to keep up with the image of the founder. My boss had many of his grandfather's weaknesses – being mean, dour, negative and insular – without many of his positives of being entrepreneurial, risk-taking and go-getting. It wasn't really his fault – the world economy and foreign exchange rates were against him. But it made it worse that he presided over the demise of his inheritance. *Management consultant and trainer*

The very rich family in the USA whom I worked for tried to create a dynasty, but the second generation was not really up for it, although they tried. Life was too easy as they didn't have to work hard to make the money as the first generation had done. *Interior designer, New York*

I worked for a wealthy entrepreneur who owned an expensive super yacht and who was a real gentleman. He didn't trust me at first but I gained his trust over time, and even though we came from totally different backgrounds we enjoyed each other's company and had mutual respect. When, sadly, he passed away and his son took over, I had to start from scratch building trust. And I realized his son was starting from scratch too, as his father had not really shared the real insights into the business with him. The son insisted on learning everything the hard way, by making mistakes, and he was the same with the yacht as with the business. So being unprepared and inheriting an empire can be quite challenging, and is not the free gift that some people see it as being. *Former Royal Navy officer*

CONCLUSION

I am a soldier who has come from the people and risen by my own efforts.

Napoleon, 1 February 1801

It was only on the evening after Lodi that I realized I was a superior being and conceived the ambition of performing great things, which hitherto had filled my thoughts only as a fantastic dream.

Napoleon, in his memoirs

In war as in politics, wasted opportunities never present themselves a second time.

Napoleon, 1803

My sword is at my side, and with it I shall go far.

Napoleon, 1794

Follow me, I am the god of the hour.

Napoleon, just before Brumaire, 1799

Soldiers, consider that from the summit of these pyramids, forty centuries look down upon you.

Napoleon's speech before Battle of Pyramids, 1798

Every French soldier carries in his cartridge-pouch the baton of a marshal of France.

Napoleon, 1802

Soldiers, I am satisfied with you.

Napoleon, 1805

Probably he was beginning to realize the hold which unbroken victory was giving him over his troops, and the demands he could make on them when he had their confidence ... with the Italian campaigns Napoleon steps on to the stage as a figure of European importance... as public opinion assumed and was encouraged to think [his victories were], simply due to the personality of the commander and to the elan of the Republican soldiers.

Markham, 1963, p34

ANALYSING NAPOLEONIC LEADERSHIP

We see Napoleon, like all leaders, as pulled in many directions, but emerging as authoritarian (even tyrannical), reluctant to accommodate differing views, and many would fear to challenge him. He would not tolerate people who resisted his grasp on power, but he envied the legitimacy enjoyed by the traditional, established crowned heads of Europe and wished he could achieve it. This was to lead to an egotistical obsession with autocracy. He was highly competitive, sought centralized leadership and dominated strategic decision making, and he made decisions quickly and determinedly.

Although taking a broad strategic view, attacking feudalism and pursuing the possibility of a united Europe, Napoleon was good at detail. Enormously energetic, he was involved in most details of his military and governmental activities. He usually took the credit for everything, although respecting the contribution of an increasingly small inner-circle of advisers and comrades-at-arms. He rewarded his supporters generously, though often they simply wanted more rewards and focused on protecting their wealth, refusing to put it at risk by following him to war again. They were to drop him like a stone when the going got tough.

Napoleon was highly visible and proactive as the leader – no quiet or behind-the-scenes leadership here. Addicted to power, he was directive, autocratic and hard-driving. He assumed that his top-down approach was the only way, expecting others to go along with his domineering leadership style and buy in to his values and vision for post-revolutionary France. His inspirational, even charismatic approach enabled him to attract a huge loyal following, even though, spendthrift with human lives, he abandoned two enormous armies at massive cost in life and *materiel*. Even soldiers who had been unpaid for months and lacked uniforms and equipment – practically volunteers – would follow him.

As a migrant himself, and coming from a poor family, Napoleon had no problem with managing a diverse group with huge variations in social class and nationality. He came to love France but he could operate any-where, exploring new territories with a keen eye for terrain and different national characteristics; but like others, he famously underestimated the challenges of invading Russia, and ruthlessly abandoned half a million men there. He sought co-operation from other rulers, and was intensely annoyed and angry by rejection from the crowned heads of Europe and their ministers. He wanted to build relationships, and was upset when his friendly overtures were turned down, although sometimes he seems not to have noticed the face-saving opportunities they offered him.

In his early military career Napoleon liked those around him to show initiative and to be themselves, and although many of his fellow-generals would probably have liked more autonomy and freedom of action, the exciting speed of his campaigns provided opportunity for the most flamboyant of warriors. But Napoleon respected the values of his more straightforward military men and, by contrast, despised most politicians. Keen on analysis and planning, he would make extensive preparations before a battle. Sometimes he could be impulsive, and he was certainly very impatient. When the government coffers were empty and raising armies and rewarding supporters had consumed all avail-able funds, he would still want to go on fighting; practical, financial considerations rarely stopped him. Often he spent his own money. He always thought, in a traditional way, that land and territories were most important, whilst his arch-enemy, England, focused on extending their colonial markets, promoting an industrial revolution and controlling global trade.

When, as Emperor, Napoleon became increasingly controlling, nervous about opposition and insecure in his ability to hang on to power, those around him – even the generals who had worked with him for years – also became nervous about doing something of which he might not approve. Aspirations for the greater good become confused with whatever would please the Emperor. He ran two sets of secret police to check on each other, and challenges to his authority were met with brutal reprisals. But there were always some of the mature diplomats and politicians around, who were alert to the fragility of his reign and working on their options as they emerged in the volatile geo-politics of Europe. Amongst them was double-agent Talleyrand, who might be described as a behind-the-scenes leader with a long-lasting influence on the Napoleonic legacy.

For over a decade and a half Napoleon dominated all aspects of the French Republic, personifying the nation, overshadowing his ministers and all around him; only Talleyrand thrived in the vacuum of power left after his first and second abdications. Napoleon leveraged his military career to gain political power at an early age. Transparent and naïve, he never sought to hide his ambition, and even his most loyal followers began to doubt his commitment to France rather than his pursuit of personal glory.

As Napoleon consolidated his power, he became unapproachable and self-absorbed. His relentlessly ambitious military strategy, at one time so inspiring, came to obscure any concern for the people who fought and suffered. Nearly half a million men perished in the snows of Russia, and as many as four million died in battle and the side-effects of war across Europe. But it was none of these factors that brought about his eventual downfall: because he had no idea how to negotiate on any basis other than military victory, the European powers had no choice but to defeat him in battle.

INSIGHTS FROM THE CAREER OF NAPOLEON

The career of Napoleon, with its ups and downs, gives us unique practical insights into the advantages and disadvantages of his approach to leadership and the background and context in which different modes of power were employed. What did he show us?

- How to get to the top – fast.

- How to build a network of supporters and choose acolytes – the dos and don'ts.

- Leaders being brilliant in their chosen area is a plus – but it may not be enough, it may only take them so far.

- Charisma, personality and constant visibility can help to secure a power base.

- Being prepared to risk everything in a sudden takeover has to be a priority.

- Seizing every opportunity offered to gain advancement in leadership and power is recommended to get on the ladder of progress, but there may come a time when consolidation is needed.

- Maintaining a power base needs control of the agenda, setting the rules, influencing all the decisions – or someone else will.

- Being intimidating and threatening – and callous of human interests – may work to a degree but can be a disaster in trying to sustain leadership and power.

- Depending on popular support and being elected to power is dangerous, as crowds are fickle.

- Trying to create a dynasty to leave a legacy depends on an appropriate successor and a stronger power base than most leaders might have.

EPILOGUE: 20 WAYS IN WHICH NAPOLEON LOST POWER AND HOW HIS WAY OF USING POWER TURNED SOUR AND COULD NOT BE SUSTAINED

1. Napoleon as First Consul, with the launch of the *Code Napoleon*, the Concordat and hundreds of economic, social and legal reforms, held out a promise of sustainable development for France – but it needed peace, and Napoleon was a soldier, and he would inevitably keep clashing with the 'triumvirate' of Austria, Russia and Prussia. His positives reforms frightened his reactionary neighbours, and he responded with war instead of negotiation, thus justifying his obsessive grip on power.

2. Napoleon came to confuse and inter-relate the future of France with his own longevity in power – especially after a series of assassination attempts in 1800, whilst he was First Consul. He ordered a crack-down on any suspected political opponents, ordered the assassination of a suspected rebel and clamped down on the press. His instincts for self-preservation, egotism and narcissism that had so effectively motivated his radical activism showed a darker side: an autocratic aversion to debate and disagreement.

3. Napoleon's desire to be adored by the masses drove him to an extraordinary act: to demand they declare their confidence in him by voting in a public plebiscite. Although he fiddled the results for the army (who hadn't voted as overwhelmingly as he thought they should), he basked in the fantasy that he represented the highest ideals of the French – over-arching the quibbles of the political class. He was thus elected First Consul for Life in 1802, a step towards

proclaiming himself Emperor in 1804, aping the dynastic monarchies of his enemies.

4. According to Machiavelli, necessary wars need to be fought; but
   there was a growing feeling that not all of Napoleon's wars were
   necessary. His compulsion to fight England – the only country he
   had not beaten conclusively – was highly personalized. The English
   press lampooned him, and he took it as a personal vendetta. It fed
   his paranoia, and he became convinced that Paris was full of spies in
   the pay of the English, all out to kill him.

5. Napoleon's ongoing conviction that he must carry on fighting battles to stay in power undermined the ability of his regime to continue
   for the long-term. Although the continued expansion of the Empire
   was welcomed by many in France (*la Gloire, l'honneur*) the economic dislocation of constant war could not be sustained, especially
   at a time when other countries, Britain in particular, were building
   capital and investing in the industrial revolution. Success in war created a temporary sense of triumph, a heady enjoyment of victory
   which could carry people along on a tide of patriotic fervour, but
   this distracted them from the lack of attention to necessary social
   and economic development, and starved the country of the necessary
   funds.

6. The other crowned heads of Europe could not tolerate Napoleon
   indefinitely; he could never be a member of their club, and the
   wars he perpetrated drained their economies. More dangerously, in
   the early years he actively promoted bourgeois revolutions in the
   countries he 'liberated'. He personified the threat of French-style revolutions in all their countries, part of the tide of rebellion that had
   already swept across the American colonies. Napoleon's France was
   not just an opponent like any other, it was toxic to the established
   social order across Europe.

7. Napoleon did try to make peace and said that he longed for a period
   of stability which could have extended his period of office, but he
   thought that peace for France could only be achieved if he was
   acknowledged as its legitimate ruler by Europe's kings and emperors. He spent huge energy and resources to make a fragile peace
   with Tsar Alexander I at Tilsit, and to become the son-in-law of the
   Austrian emperor. He expected them both to admit him as their peer,
   and was surprised when they did not. While all this was going on,
   and without Napoleon's appreciation, some of the greatest diplomatic manipulators (like Metternich) were piecing together a new
   Europe, made up of new states that used but transcended the old
   empires and princedoms.

8. Napoleon's loyalty to his family members amounted to squandering his powers of patronage. Appointing them to rule kingdoms across Europe, they often showed themselves to be incompetent or self-seeking, or both. Mostly they were no better than the often-corrupt monarchs they replaced. This was surely an occasion for meritocracy, to create a cadre of new talent inspired by revolutionary ideals and dependent on him. But he used his powers of patronage simply to reward his family, because personal loyalty had become the primary virtue.

9. When he rewarded his favourite generals with appointments to leadership roles in his over-extended Empire, they too often took this as a kind of pension rather than an appointment to the front-line of the Revolution. It seemed to be the case that the ruling elite became absorbed in preserving their own privileges.

10. Napoleon always struggled to delegate, and seemed to be a poor judge of talent and potential loyalty. His system of patronage often backfired on him and further undermined his efforts to rule a very large operation, forcing him to rely on his own prodigious personal efforts, leading to complete exhaustion. Trusting no one leads to isolation, an obsession with control, the perceived need to spy on others and being on guard 24/7.

11. The creation of new countries and borders, such as the Grand Duchy of Warsaw to replace the truncated Poland, the Confederation of the Rhine, the Cisalpine Republic, anticipated the new order of Europe half a century later, but were ahead of their time and on a collision course with the 'triumvirate' of Russia, Austria and Prussia. Directly confronting the most powerful usually ends with being knocked back.

12. The birth of Napoleon's son and heir, the King of Rome, in March 1811 after his marriage to Marie-Louise, Archduchess of Austria, was met with great rejoicing. Had the young man been older when Napoleon finally abdicated, had he not been an Austrian Prince, had Napoleon died in battle, then he might have had a chance to become Napoleon II. But this possibility was hardly even considered – his father's legitimacy rested too much on force. When he lost at Waterloo, it all tumbled down.

13. The invasion of Russia must be seen as one of the main turning points in Napoleon's attempts at creating a long-term tenure of leadership. How often can a leader lose nearly half a million soldiers and survive? Even though he blamed the calamity on unseasonably bad weather and appeared to survive this reversal politically, he lost a generation of loyal, able and experienced soldiers. When he fought again it was with raw young conscripts, and he struggled to replace the horses and artillery he had lost. It is remarkable that he survived

the campaign himself, and that he clung onto political power for another two years is a real testament to his tenacity and grip on French politics.

14. The enormity of the disaster of the retreat from Moscow gave encouragement and inspiration to Napoleon's enemies – he was no longer unbeatable. This episode was followed by a string of military defeats that were eventually to lead to his downfall. Once the momentum of success is broken, winning becomes more of a struggle. The effect of a defeat after an almost unbroken string of victories is to admit doubt and insecurity, both of which are hard to overcome in war.

15. In January 1814, anti-French coalition armies entered France, and Paris was captured without a fight by combined enemy forces two months later. This would appear to have been the result of three factors: Napoleon's declining military prowess with the loss of his army in Russia; the growing confidence and co-ordination amongst the 'triumvirate' of Russia, Austria and Prussia; and the reluctance of Parisians to risk their city and their lives in a violent defence. Napoleon was removed from power and exiled to Elba. But he continued to rule there, and plotted a comeback. Maybe he was in denial of his loss: the balance of power had shifted, and France faced a new alignment of forces. Already others in Paris were looking to post-Napoleonic settlements. Only Napoleon and a few loyal friends persisted in the fantasy that the future of France was inseparable from that of 'General Bonaparte'.

16. The political machinery supporting Napoleon's power proved inadequate at the crucial moment when occupying forces removed Napoleon's wife and son from Paris. Had his brother Joseph taken the reigns as intended, there may not have been a vacuum so readily filled by Louis XVIII, a Bourbon family member hastily restored to the French throne. The failure of Napoleon's network of patronage at the crucial moment suggests the weakness of this network all along – it could not survive adversity.

17. Some say it was pusillanimity on the part of Napoleon's ministers that enabled the Bourbon restoration. But key ministers like Talleyrand had long been playing both sides, foreseeing the growing power of the allies and their desire for stability in France. The rapid replacement of Napoleon with Louis XVII suited many interests now that Napoleon was marginalized and everyone wanted peace.

18. Exiled on the island of Elba, Napoleon hoped for a come-back, planned for it and, amazingly, pulled it off. But France was reeling under the dislocation of decades of war and desperate for peace. If

the populace had wanted Napoleon to stay, they might have fought harder to keep out the Allies when they invaded. But the continuous effort of following a charismatic leader to victory in the field was suddenly too dissonant with the reality. When the charismatic leader was no longer there in person, the drive for victory evaporated with the belief in its possibility.

19. Napoleon could still make a great show of personal charisma and opportunism, and indeed was able to raise an army and force Louis XVIII to flee from Paris, but the strength of the Allies and the loss of the French army in Russia undermined Napoleon's ability to keep fighting, and fighting was the only way he knew to get his Empire back.

20. Napoleon really only got the message that he had lost everything when he was forced to abdicate for the second time to the much more distant and inhospitable island of St Helena; but there he focused on rewriting history, convincing himself that he could have carried on, if only – the loss of power can be an almost impossible burden to bear for one who lived so devotedly by it.

EPILOGUE, CONTINUED: WHAT NAPOLEON CAN TELL US ABOUT HOW POWER WORKS IN ORGANIZATIONS AND SOCIETY

Organizations and societies need continuity and periods of time without constant upheaval, in order to consolidate change and achieve sustainable development. Change- and action-obsessed leaders, especially those operating opportunistically through a seizure of power, maintaining their power through fear and manipulation, cannot last indefinitely. But they can hurt a lot of people on the way.

Heavy-handed control by a self-obsessed leader, accompanied by a crackdown on suspected rivals and any forms of dissent or disagreement, can push opposition underground; but it may then increase, and it will certainly lead to widespread discontent and explode at some point. Leaders interested only in their own personal status and obsessed with developing dynastic power tend to neglect the development of their organizations and countries in preference to actions which secure their power base.

The tolerance of personal vendettas and acts of revenge in organizations and societies (especially perpetuated by paranoid leaders) is ultimately destructive, and people live in fear and isolation. Constant expansion by takeovers – of other companies by another, and of invasions of countries by another – can create a temporary sense of triumph, a heady enjoyment of victory which can carry the victors along on a tide of loyalty and patriotic fervour, but this distracts them from normal development processes and is often used to divert attention from deep-seated problems.

When organizations and societies undergo revolutionary change and experience major shifts in power sources, this creates fear and discomfort in those that are more stable, whose leaders are more conservative and who are not ready for change. It can be difficult for organizations and societies that have undergone revolutionary change and shifts in power to settle down and enjoy a period of stability; they will not be trusted by their competitors and neighbours, who will always be on the look-out for new revolutions and power-grabs.

Organizations and societies tend to develop power elites which do them no favours: they can be self-seeking, corrupt and disloyal to all but their immediate associates and do little for the organization or society itself. When the power elite idealizes itself as a meritocracy, it can lead to competition and in-fighting over who should be the next leader, over and above everyone else. Merit can be a good route to promotion, but it is seldom enough to keep hold of power.

Leaders of organizations and societies who try to run everything by themselves, trusting no one, can become isolated, develop an obsession with control, feel the need to spy on others – and cannot last forever. Some organizations and societies are so progressive that they are ahead of their time, and therefore on a collision course with the old order who will close ranks against them. This is especially so when they throw out old ways of legitimizing power, because they implicitly question the vested interests of those who benefit from inequality. Many leaders of organizations and societies who come from unconventional origins, very different from those in the past, find that the foundations of their legitimacy can be too fragile and are forced out. How often can leaders of organizations and societies face a self-created major reversal, a huge disaster, and survive? Can they carry on if they try to blame it on outside factors? This failure eats away at the foundation of their power and they lose credibility. Leaders need to protect resources to maintain power, or can quickly lose influence along with the resources they have lost.

A reversal suffered at the hands of a competitor or an enemy obviously not only reduces the power of the loser but increases the empowerment of the winner and gives the competitor or enemy much more confidence as a result.

Some leaders can be removed from power as the result of a reversal, but remain in denial of this loss. They want to make a come-back, and some manage it; often they thereby become more conservative forces, preventing further change and development.

A network of patronage needs careful maintenance, and frequent renewal. An elite group of cronies, well-entrenched, will prevent further change, unless constantly reminded of the need for loyalty and action. A complacent network, however close to power, will be loyal only when the going is good. Intransigence on the part of the leadership group as a whole can lead to chaos and collapse. One of the problems when a leader plays one side against another is that everyone has to join in the game, destroying collaboration, learning and innovation. Everything is reduced to a fight for survival.

When enthusiasm for a charismatic leader evaporates, there can be a huge sense of relief at an opportunity to relax and realize what's going on. When the charismatic leader is no longer there in person, the drive for whatever it is he or she wants suddenly disappears.

Some leaders have only one way of operating and one vision, and when circumstances change they are swept away; often control then reverts to canny negotiators doing one deal at a time, rather than those with the single powerful vision.

Leaders try to rewrite history, convincing themselves that they could have carried on being leaders, if only; the loss of power can be an almost impossible burden to bear for one who lived or died by it, and they struggle to understand their own part in its loss.

SUMMARISING NAPOLEONIC LEADERSHIP

- As a supporter of the Revolution, Napoleon was seen as modern, new worldly, anti-feudal, anti-aristocratic – but ahead of his time, and he over-estimated the popularity of new ideas.

- He was ambitious, even to the extent of going to the very top.

- He had an underprivileged start in life and then obsessively tried to compensate for it.

- His action was speedy, rapid, flexible, urgent, to the extent of pushing hard to overcome any resistance, and not always listening to warnings.

- Napoleon was hands-on, even controlling.

- Hard-working, energetic, ever present, involved in all aspects of leadership and management.

- Well-prepared, precise and exact, to the extent of managing everything in front of as well as behind the scenes.

- Egotistical, even narcissistic.

- Practical, straightforward, calm and unsentimental, even to the point of being callous about human and personal issues.

- Surprisingly naïve, to the extent of over-simplicity and overconfidence that everything is possible.

- Eager to be liked, even to the extent of rewarding flattery and loyalty more than competence.

- Critical of others and with an attitude of superiority, demanding respect but not willing to give it to others.

- Wanting praise to the extent of being intolerant of criticism and not realizing the damage caused by an absence of feedback.

- Obsessed with the need for the constant demonstration of ability, even to the detriment of the organization.

Napoleon's approach to leadership provides colourful examples of how to gain and use power on the battlefield, in domestic politics and in the international scene – and in the workplace. He provides examples that are applicable to our own less turbulent times, because the demands on leaders are just as complex and multifaceted. Strengths of Napoleonic leadership can include brilliance in a chosen field, charisma, fearlessness, adventurousness, confidence, energy, determination, passion, being visionary, and having excellent planning and organizing skills. But these can have a shadow side, such as his need for constant acclaim, demanding adulation, callously wasting resources, being too egotistical and narcissistic, being overly-controlling and autocratic, manipulative, obsessive, naïve, assuming constant success and support and focusing on self-preserving behaviours. But more important than these personal traits are the ideologies that he and others turned to in order to legitimize his power: patronage, meritocracy, charisma, opportunism, manipulation, coercion, popularity and succession – and this has been our focus here.

BIBLIOGRAPHY

NAPOLEON

Abbott, J. (2005). *Life of Napoleon Bonaparte*. New York: Kessinger.

Addey, K. (1983). *Napoleon*. London: Evergreen Lives.

Alexander, R.S. (2001). *Napoleon*. London: Arnold.

Amini, I. (2000). *Napoleon and Persia*. New York: Taylor & Francis.

Aronson, T. (1990). *Napoleon and Josephine: A love story*. London: John Murray.

Bell, D.A. (2005). Napoleon in the flesh. *MLN*, *20*(4), 711–715.

Blaufarb, R. (2007). *Napoleon: Symbol for an age, a brief history with documents*. London: Bedford.

Boycott-Brown, M. (2001). *The Road to Rivoli: Napoleon's first campaign*. London: Cassell.

Broers, M. (2005). *The Napoleonic Empire in Italy, 1796–1814: Cultural imperialism in a European context?* London: Palgrave Macmillan.

Butterfield, H. (1939). *Napoleon*. *Great Lives*. London: Duckworth.

Byman, D.L. and Pollack, K.M. (2001). Let us now praise great men: Bringing the statesman back in. *International Security*, *25*(4), 107–146.

Chandler, D. (1995). *The Campaigns of Napoleon*. New York: Simon & Schuster.

Chandler, D. (2002). *Napoleon*. New York: Leo Cooper.

Charles-Roux, F. (1937). *Bonaparte: Governor of Egypt*. London: Methuen.

Chesney, C. (2006). *Waterloo Lectures: A study of the campaign of 1815*. New York: Kessinger.

Cohen, J.M. & M.J. (1960). *The Penguin Dictionary of Quotations*. Harmondsworth: Penguin.

Connelly, O. (2006). *Blundering to Glory: Napoleon's military campaigns*. New York: Rowman & Littlefield.

Cordingly, D. (2004). *The Billy Ruffian: The Bellerophon and the downfall of Napoleon*. London: Bloomsbury.

Cronin, V. (1971). *Napoleon*. London: History Book Club.

Dwyer, P.G. (2001). Napoleon and the drive for glory: Reflections on the making of French foreign policy. In Dwyer, P.G., *Napoleon and Europe* (pp. 118–135). London: Longman.

Dwyer, P.G. (2002). From Corsican nationalist to French revolutionary: Problems of identity in the writings of the young Napoleon, 1785–1793. *French History*, *16*(2), 132–152.

Dwyer, P.G. (2004). Napoleon Bonaparte as hero and saviour: Image, rhetoric and behaviour in the construction of a legend. *French History*, *18*(4), 379–403.

Dwyer, P.G. (2007). *Napoleon: The path to power, 1769–1799*. London: Bloomsbury.

Englund, S. (2004). *Napoleon: A political life*. New York: Scribner.

Fremont-Barnes, G. and Fisher, T. (2004). *The Napoleonic Wars: The rise and fall of an empire*. London: Osprey.

Gallo, M. (1997a). *Napoleon, The Sun of Austerlitz*. London: Macmillan.

Gallo, M. (1997b). *Napoleon, The Song of Departure*. London: Macmillan.

Gallo, M. (2005). *Napoleon, The Emperor of Kings*. London: Macmillan.

Gates, D. (2003). *The Napoleonic Wars, 1803–1815*. London: Pimlico.

Geyl, P. (1949). *Napoleon: For and against*. London: Bain.

Glenn, P.F. (2001). Nietzsche's Napoleon: The higher man as political actor. *The Review of Politics, 63*(1), 129–158.

Goetz, R. (2005). *1805: Austerlitz: Napoleon and the destruction of the third coalition*. New York: Greenhill.

Haythornthwaite, P.J. (1995). *The Napoleonic Source Book*. London: Arms and Armour.

Hazareesingh, S. (2004). *The Legend of Napoleon*. Cambridge: Granta.

Johnson, P. (2002). *Napoleon: A life*. London: Penguin.

Johnson, P. (2003). *Napoleon*. London: Weidenfeld & Nicolson.

Kennedy, C. (2005). No more heroes. *The Director*, (Jan.), 46–48.

Kroll, M.J., Toombs, L.A. and Wright, P. (2000). Napoleon's tragic march home from Moscow: Lessons in hubris. *Academy of Management Executive, 14*(1), 117–128.

Markham, F. (1963). *Napoleon*. New York: Mentor.

Martin, A. (2000). *Napoleon the Novelist*. Cambridge: Polity.

McLynn, F. (1998). *Napoleon: A biography*. London: Pimlico.

Palmer, A. (1998). *An Encyclopedia of Napoleon's Europe*. London: Constable.

Palmer, A.W. (1962). *A Dictionary of Modern History, 1789–1945*. Harmondsworth: Penguin.

Parker, H.T. (1987). Napoleon reconsidered: An invitation to inquiry and reflection. *French Historical Studies, 15*(1), 142–156.

Roberts, A. (2001). *Napoleon and Wellington*. London: Weidenfeld & Nicholson.

Schom, A. (1998). *Napoleon Bonaparte*. London: Harper Perennial.

Schwarzfuchs, S. (1979). *Napoleon, the Jews and the Sanhedrin*. London: Routledge.

Semmel, S. (2004). *Napoleon and the British*. New Haven, CT: Yale University Press.

Stathern, P. (2007). *Napoleon in Egypt: The greatest glory*. London: Jonathan Cape.

Stiles, A. (1990). *Napoleon, France and Europe*. London: Hodder & Stoughton.

Tulard, J. (1984). *Napoleon: The myth of the saviour*. London: Methuen.

Woloch, I. (2001). *Napoleon and His Collaborators: The making of a dictatorship*. New York: Norton.

Woodward, C. (2005). Napoleon's last journey. *History Today, 55*(7).

Zamoyski, A. (2004). *1812: Napoleon's fatal march on Moscow*. London: HarperCollins.

Zamoyski, A. (2008). *Rites of Peace: The fall of Napoleon and the Congress of Vienna*. London: Harper Perennial.

LEADERSHIP AND POWER

Dahl, R.A. (1957). The concept of power. *Behavioral Science, 2*, 210–215.

Drucker, P.F. (1974). *Management Tasks, Responsibilities and Practices*. New York: Harper and Row.

Emerson, R.M. (1962). Power dependence relations. *American Sociological Review, 27*, 31–41.

Fleming, P. and Spicer, A. (2014). Power in management and organization science. *The Academy of Management Annals, 8*(1), 237–298.

Gosling, J., Jones, S., Sutherland, I. and Dijkstra, J. (2012). *Key Concepts in Leadership*. London: Sage.

Grint, K. (2014). 'The hedgehog and the fox: Leadership lessons from D-Day'. *Leadership, 10*(2), 240–260.

Jones, S. and Gosling, J. (2005). *Nelson's Way: Leadership lessons from the great commander*. London: Nicholas Brealey.

Latour, B. (1986). The power of association, in power, action and belief: A new sociology of knowledge?. *Sociological Review Monograph, 32*, 264–280.

McClelland, D.C. and Burnham, D.H. (1976). Power is the great motivator. *Harvard Business Review, 54*, 100–110.

Mintzberg, H. (1963). *The Nature of Managerial Work*. New York: Harper & Row.

Parker, L.D. (1984). Control in organizational life: The contribution of Mary Parker Follett. *Academy of Management Review, 9*, 736–745.

Pettigrew, A.M. (1972). Information control as a power resource. *Sociology, 6*, 187–204.

Pettigrew, A.M. (1973). *The Politics of Organizational Decision Making*. London: Tavistock.

Pfeffer, J. (1981). *Power in Organizations*. Boston, MA: Pitman.

Salancik, G.R. and Pfeffer, J. (1974). The bases and uses of power in organizational decision making. *Administrative Science Quarterly, 19*, 453–473.

Stahl, M.J. (1983). Achievement, power and managerial motivation: Selecting managerial talent with the job choice exercise. *Personnel Psychology, 36*, 775–789.

Vrendenburgh, D.J. and Maurer, J.G. (1984). A process framework of organizational politics. *Human Relations, 37*, 47–66.

Widmer, H. (1980). Business lessons from military strategy. *McKinsey Quarterly, 2*, 59–67.

Winter, D.G. (1973). *The Power Motive*. New York: Free Press.

Yukl, G. and Falbe, C.M. (1991). The importance of different power sources in downward and lateral relations. *Journal of Applied Psychology, 76*, 416–423.

INDEX